100 DIVERSE VOICES

100 DIVERSE VOICES ON PARENTHOOD

Ideas, advice, and anecdotes
for new parents.

ABOUT THE BOOK.

This book cannot tell you how to raise your baby, because no one can tell you how to do that.

In fact, a lot of the authors who share their stories in the pages of this book say things like, "Do what's best for your baby," and, "Go with what works for your family," because when it comes to raising a little human, there are no fail-safe instructions. This book is meant to be a supplemental guide to your own inner voice, your gut, and the relationship you build with your baby as they grow. It's meant to be a reassuring reminder that it's okay to do it the old-school way, or the new way you just made up, or the way your baby likes it, or the way your doctor told you to do it. It's meant to be a reminder that the parenting community is huge, and no matter what those parents look like or where they come from, we all share a united goal—to raise happy, thriving humans.

To create this book, we asked over one hundred people to share their stories and advice for parents who are navigating the very first year of parenthood. The authors in this book are not writers, and most of them are not experts who have studied parenting or child development. They are simply people who have raised babies and learned something valuable along the way. Some stories are about things almost all new parents identify with, like breastfeeding, or diaper bags, or screen time. Other stories are about things not every parent experiences, like how to navigate caring for a sick baby, or how to manage parenthood after a separation or divorce.

Most of all this book is meant to encourage the idea that community matters. Its intent is to provide good information and to lay the foundation for the concept of community you will bring to your new life as a parent caring for your child.

Printed in the United States of America.

A Kids Book About books are available online: akidsco.com
To share your stories, ask questions, or inquire about bulk
purchases (schools, libraries, and nonprofits), please use
the following email address: *hello@akidsco.com*

www.akidsco.com

ISBN: 978-1-953955-21-0

Designed by Rick DeLucco
Edited by Ashley Simpo, Emma Wolf, Wynn Rankin,
Denise Morales Soto, and Jennifer Goldstein

Dedicated to every new parent hoping to foster
a better future for the next generation.

CONTENTS.

SECTION ONE
THE BIG PICTURE.

1.	**Raising an Anti-racist Baby** by Tabitha St. Bernard-Jacobs	30
2.	**Letting Them Pave the Way** by Orly Agai Marley	34
3.	**Misinformation** by Dr. Mona Amin	36
4.	**Building Parenting Skills** by Jessi Duley	38
5.	**Gender Expectations** by Noleca Anderson Radway	42
6.	**How Vaccines Work** by Dr. Malia Jones, PhD	44
7.	**Sense of Purpose** by Emmitt Smith	48
8.	**Raising a Mixed-race Child** by Dr. Jennifer Noble, PhD	50
9.	**Present vs. Future Needs** by LaToia Levy Johnson	52
10.	**Attachment Parenting** by Evelyn Yang	56
11.	**Day-to-Day Fears** by Gearah Goldstein	58
12.	**Living with Your Parent** by Rachael Lucille Van Klompenberg	60
13.	**Two Worldviews** by David Kim	62
14.	**When Your Child Is Really Sick** by Jen and Ruben Alvarado	64
15.	**Learning Alongside Your Child** by Denise Woodard	66
16.	**Humor** by Elizabeth Stock	68
17.	**Expect the Unexpected** by Kyle Steed	70
18.	**Moral Responsibility** by Zola Ellen	72
19.	**Our Money Stories** by Georgia Lee Hussey	76
20.	**Free Range(ish) Parenting** by Onikah Asamoa-Caesar	80
21.	**Raising a Curious Child** by Ara Katz	82
22.	**Choices Around Equity** by Stephen Green	86

CONTENTS CONT.

SECTION TWO
THE BABY.

23. **Questions for the Doctor** by Dr. Tracey Agnese — 90

24. **Diapering** by Altimese Nichole — 98

25. **Car Seats** by Ryan Tillman — 102

26. **Screens** by Anya Kamenetz — 106

27. **Go Outside** by Paul J. Pastor — 108

28. **Swaddling** by Rick DeLucco — 110

29. **Communication Before Language** by Cherie Ulmer — 112

30. **Dental Care** by Vanessa Coupet, DMD — 114

31. **Bottle Feeding** by D.L. Mayfield — 118

32. **Nurturing** by Ethan Thrower — 120

33. **Play and Development** by Jennifer White-Johnson — 122

34. **Language Acquisition** by Shari Harpaz — 124

35. **A Doctor's Note** by Dr. Raphael Sharon — 126

36. **Feeding Twins** by Ashley Countryman — 134

37. **Breastfeeding** by Marie Rocha — 136

38. **Tummy Time** by Lindsey Lewis — 140

39. **Watching TV** by Dr. Michele Foss-Snowden, PhD — 142

40. **Milestones** by Suzy Ultman — 144

41. **Baby's First Night on Their Own** by Bryan Wolf — 146

42. **Gut Health** by Dr. Tasneem "Dr. Taz" Bhatia — 148

43. **Breast Milk Banks** by Alisa Norman — 152

44. **Poop!** by Jay Leary — 154

45. **Newborn Essentials** by Sarah Gould Steinhardt and Juliet Fuisz — 156

46. **Nighttime Routine** by Nabil Zerizef — 158

47. **Feeding Your Baby** by Ria Ghosh and Rohit Goel — 160

48. **The Perfect* Diaper Bag** by Doug Cornett — 162

49. **Creative Interaction** by Ahlam Soliman — 164

CONTENTS CONT.

50. **Sleep Training** by Natalie Willes   166

51. **Babywearing** by Jeremy Daniel   168

52. **The Changing Station** by Kelly DeLucco   170

53. **Reading Books** by Jelani Memory   172

SECTION THREE
EVERYONE ELSE.

54. **Social Media** by Conz Preti   176

55. **Boundaries for Family** by Myleik Teele   178

56. **How to Involve Family** by Jennifer A. Perry   180

57. **Letting Family Help** by Jucel Erroba   182

58. **Finding Community** by Karney Dunah   184

59. **Combatting Comparison** by Sylvia Farbstein   188

60. **New Social Reality** by Lauren Winfrey   192

61. **Possessiveness** by Megan Laney   194

62. **Living Far Away** by Tiffany Rose Smith   196

63. **Anti-shame Parenting Pillars** by Dominique Matti   198

64. **Finding Care** by Charnaie Gordon   200

65. **Siblings** by Kherri Jean   202

66. **Babysitters** by Yasmin Fathi   204

67. **Physical Boundaries** by Qimmah Saafir   206

SECTION FOUR
YOU, TOO.

68. **Navigating Your Feelings** by Dr. Becky Kennedy   210

69. **The Juggle** by Joy Cho   212

70. **Staying Connected** by Rozanda "Chilli" Thomas   214

71. **Parenting Ourselves** by Kileah McIlvain   216

72. **Single Parents Returning to Work** by Ashley Simpo   218

73. **The Choice to Have (Only) One** by Jose Corona   222

74. **Self-care** by Dr. Ann-Louise Lockhart, PsyD   224

CONTENTS CONT.

75. **Arguments** by Jonathan Simcoe 226

76. **Parenting Roles**
    by Rebecca Gitlitz-Rapoport and Sam Rapoport 230

77. **Postpartum Depression** by Patricia A. White 234

78. **Postpartum Depression for Dads** by Joel Leon 236

79. **Preparedness** by Jendayi Smith 238

80. **Stay-at-home Parent** by Wynn Rankin 240

81. **Divorce** by Simona Foasade Silah 242

82. **Anxiety After Baby** by Dr. Cassidy Freitas, PhD 244

83. **Co-parenting** by Tranette Martin 248

84. **Overcoming Frustration** by Matthew C. Winner 252

85. **Introducing Yourself to Baby** by Jess Teutonico 256

86. **Parenting Groups** by Sherisa de Groot 258

87. **Documenting Firsts** by Harold Hughes 260

88. **Overcoming Overwhelm** by Tejal Patel 262

89. **Single Parenting From a Dad's POV** by Brett Moore 264

90. **Preserving Your Relationship**
    by Pastor Keyonn Anthony Wright-Sheppard Sr. 266

91. **Mindfulness** by Michael Booth 268

92. **Postpartum Support** by Kayla Cushner, CNM 272

93. **Division of Labor** by Kirby Winfield 276

94. **Asking for Help** by Sarah Beck 280

95. **Return to Work** by Sara Scott-Curran 282

96. **Traveling with Baby** by Tanya Hayles 284

97. **The Journey of Single Parenthood** by Hilary Powers 288

98. **New Family Dynamics** by Maurice Cowley 290

99. **Body Empowerment** by Elle Pierre 292

100. **Mental Health** by Homero Radway 294

ABOUT THE EDITORS.

Ashley Simpo (she/her) is a writer and author born and raised in Northern California, now living in Brooklyn, New York, and working as managing editor at CRWNMAG. She has penned multiple essays for digital and print and is featured in *Marie Claire*, *The New York Times*, MOTHER TONGUE, *Essence*, *Huffington Post*, and *Parents* magazine. Ashley is also the author of *A Kids Book About Divorce* and has lent her voice to podcasts and publications, sharing her insight on how families can heal after separation. She is divorced, partnered, and happily co-parenting her kid, Orion (he/them).

As a seasoned writer and editor, Ashley was especially excited to work with the authors of this book and help them tell their unique stories. Oftentimes, these stories required a great deal of trust and safety in order to be shared, which grounded the process in acceptance. She approached each story as a form of community building and truth-telling—revealing the commonalities between all parents, no matter who they are.

Emma Wolf (she/her) is a book editor at the kids media company, A Kids Co. She was raised in the Portland metro area in a house full of books and became a voracious reader at an early age. Emma graduated from the University of Oregon in 2019 with a BA in journalism and from Portland State University in 2021 with an MA in book publishing. Emma lives in Portland, Oregon, and in her free time enjoys snuggling up with a book and her cat Milky Way, drinking kombucha, and spending time with friends and family hiking and enjoying the beauty of the Pacific Northwest.

While Emma considers herself to be far from parenthood, she immensely enjoyed working on this project and learning from the incredible group of parents and caregivers featured in this book. To her, the most impactful aspect of this work has been cultivating a widely diverse group of voices to speak to parenting, all from varied backgrounds, perspectives, and parenthood dynamics. The joy of being an editor is being entrusted with a writer's vulnerability on paper, and Emma extends her sincerest gratitude to all the loving parents who showed up with so much honesty and empathy to create something powerful for the next generation of parents.

Jennifer Goldstein (she/her) is head of books at the kids media company, A Kids Co. She was born and raised in Tulsa, Oklahoma, and has deep roots in the farming community of Garfield, Kansas, where her parents were born and raised. Jennifer learned from her family that women can drive tractors *and* raise babies. Today, she lives north of Chicago with her wife and younger son— their eldest is off on his own now. She's been in publishing since she graduated from the University of Kansas with a BA in history.

Jennifer still has lots to learn in this life and is honored to work on this project. She's made books for kids for many years, but this is her first book for parents. Talking with so many parents, caregivers, aunts, uncles, and grandparents for this project and working with them on their stories reminds her that out of many, we are one humanity.

Wynn Rankin (he/him) is a freelance editor and full-time dad, raising two sons with his husband in Portland, Oregon. He's helped shape stories and experiences at Apple, Chronicle Books, Warner Bros., and Cranium.

As a proud gay and stay-at-home dad, Wynn was thrilled to work with this collection of families, editors, and the A Kids Co. team. Parenting is an emotional and complicated experience that is as unique as every person who does it, so it was a distinct pleasure to help amplify such a diverse set of voices. He was awaiting the birth of his second child during the development of this book, and his firsthand experience in finding strength within this community is something he's particularly proud to share with you.

INTRODUCTION.

I like to say that being a dad is the one superpower I was born with. There was no need for a radioactive spider to bite me, a wizard to gift me mystical powers, or to have an intergalactic peace-keeping ring on my finger. I knew how to do it, in my bones, as soon as I had my first kid. The instincts just kicked in for me. You want to protect them, cuddle them, and give up everything to make sure they have what they need. If that's not a superpower, then I don't know what is.

But I'm not unique.

I think all parents have this superpower deep inside. There are those things that you just know, as a parent, you were made to do.

Now, no one ever said being a superhero was easy, and being a parent is no different. In fact, it's pretty hard. I have six kids who are part of a blended family—I started with one, added four new ones, and then had one more. My kids are a wild bunch, and each is complex in their own unique way. I love all of my kids, and while I truly feel like I was made to do this, I'm far from perfect at it. In fact, being a parent is the hardest thing I've ever done, and it turns out, most parents agree with me.

But here's the good news: we weren't made to do it alone. Ever heard the saying, "It takes a village to raise a child."? We need that village to lean on, ask advice from, help us discover new skills, keep us away from unnecessary mistakes, and encourage us to believe that we do indeed know how to do this.

This book is that village.

One hundred diverse voices offering up their wisdom, advice, tips, encouragement, stories, and cautionary tales for new parents like you. And we took great pains to make sure this was the most diverse parenting book out there.

The contributors to this book truly represent a diverse range of experiences. Inside you'll find a collective of families with all kinds of parenting journeys. Not only are the stories shared inclusive of all kinds of parenting, but all kinds of people. We've asked young parents, Black parents like myself, parents who've adopted, single parents, activist parents, parents of kids with disabilities, LGBTQIA+ parents, pediatricians, midwives, licensed clinical social workers, dentists, doulas, speech therapists, and every other kind of parent, professional, and caring individual you can imagine to be that village for parents just like you.

As you turn the pages of this book, you'll notice every author bio contains a bit of information about each author's identity— their lived experience, pronouns, nationality, race, relationship status, what their families look like, and more. This information is included intentionally to ground their stories in their most important truths, who they are, and how they see the world. But also, to remind us all, that we can learn so much from those who have backgrounds and experiences different from our own.

It matters because for most people, the advice they get about parenting comes from people who look and live like them, and that's okay. But we think everything is better when we can learn, not just from the people we're familiar with, but from the people we might never think to ask. As you get to know the folks in this book, you'll find no matter what their demographic are, their stories are incredibly relatable, inspiring, and encouraging. You'll learn a little bit about different cultures, different ways of life, different life experiences, and how similar we all actually are, especially when it comes to how we love and raise our kids.

Like Cherie Ulmer, a child of deaf parents (or CODA), and a child development specialist for deaf and hard of hearing students, who wrote about communicating with your baby through words, actions, and sign language. Or Doug Cornett, a teacher and dad of two, who shared his description of the perfect diaper bag (hint: it doesn't exist). And Tabitha St.

Bernard-Jacobs, a Trinidadian American immigrant, mother, writer, organizer, and one of the founding members of the Women's March, who writes about raising an anti-racist baby. Or Marie Rocha, a Black venture capital investor, who talks about whether breastfeeding is right for you as a new mom.

Each chapter in this book is as unique as its author and the kids they learned to care for. We gathered these folks together to create the proverbial village for new parents during the frenzy of the first year of parenthood. Use this as a handy guide to sit with for five minutes or an hour, between feedings, after baby goes to sleep, to extract useful information and much-needed encouragement.

You can read this book from cover to cover, or you can skip around to the parts that matter most to you. But whichever chapters you read, remember the stories told are real, that they were shared with an incredible amount of vulnerability, and that every single person who contributed to this book had you and your new baby in mind.

These authors also recognize there are some really big and difficult things that come with parenting, which we didn't want to gloss over or ignore. Some of those topics include raising an anti-racist kid and discussions about gender, divorce, SIDS, among others. Day-to-day parenting has its challenges, and for some parents, those challenges can feel nearly insurmountable at times. These authors are here for you and see you in that struggle. You are not alone.

In the pages of this book are the stories of people who know that parenting isn't easy. But just because it feels hard, doesn't mean you weren't born with the superpower to do it. The parents in this book have made mistakes, learned lessons, found creative ways to pivot, and done the impossible...raise a child.

So, welcome, fellow parent. I hope what you find here reminds you that even in the most overwhelming moments of your first year of parenthood, you're not alone.

Jelani Memory
Founder and CEO of A Kids Co.

DIVERSITY.

This section lays out how the 100 diverse voices who contributed to this book describe their identity and experience. The words chosen are their own. As you read, you'll find more background throughout the book and accompanying each of the chapters.

RACIAL & ETHNIC DIVERSITY

Black
Native American
Gaelic
Hispanic
Afro Latina
Hispanic & Irish
Asian
Latina/Latino
West Indian
Jewish
Arab American
Indian
Caucasian
Haitian American
Korean

Biracial
White
African American
Jamaican
Magyar
Pacific Islander
Middle Eastern
Egyptian
Black & Latino

RELATIONSHIP DIVERSITY

Married
Divorced
Separated
Divorced & Remarried
Domestic
Polyamorous
Partnership
Single

Divorcing
Married & Divorced
Life Partner

SEXUAL ORIENTATION DIVERSITY

Heterosexual
Queer
Bisexual
Questioning
Fluid
Gay

GENDER DIVERSITY

Cisgender Female
Female
Femme
Cisgender Male
Male
Non-Binary
Transgender Female

HEALTH AND DISABILITY DIVERSITY

Autistic

Dyslexia

Epilepsy

Neurodivergent

Speech Impediment

ADHD

Kidney Failure/
Dialysis

Graves Disease

Depression

AGE DIVERSITY

Under Age 30

Ages 30-35

Ages 36-40

Ages 41-50

Ages 51-60

Ages 60+

INCOME DIVERSITY

Public Assistance
$0-45K
$45-75K
$75K
$100K+

EDUCATION DIVERSITY

Doctor of Medicine
GED
High School
 Graduate
Juris Doctorate
Some College
Master's Degree
PhD
Doctor of Medicine
 in Dentistry
Trade School
Air Force Degree

Associate's Degree
Bachelor's Degree

LOCATION DIVERSITY

Alabama

California

Connecticut

Florida

Georgia

Illinois

Maine

Maryland

Michigan

Minnesota

New Jersey

New Mexico

New York

Ohio

Oklahoma

Oregon

Pennsylvania

South Carolina

Texas

Virginia

Washington

Wisconsin

Canada

The Netherlands

SECTION ONE
THE BIG PICTURE.

As difficult as it is to believe now, babies will be adults. As soon as they're born, they start to learn and evolve into the people they'll be tomorrow. Their environment and the choices you make as parents have incredible power over who they turn out to be and how they will impact the world. Mindfulness and awareness should start as early as possible.

Every parent has that one thing they look back on and wonder, Could I have done that differently? The answer is often yes, because we learn more about our kids and our world as we gain experience. In this section of the book, you'll hear from parents, caregivers, and experts who tackle some tough topics—everything from approaching race and gender to how you manage frustration and anger. We encourage you to use the following chapters to engage in conversations with your partner and community so you can make informed decisions about your future grown-up.

Chapter 1

RAISING AN ANTI-RACIST BABY.

It's never too early to start.

Tabitha St. Bernard-Jacobs is a Trinidadian American immigrant, mother, writer, organizer, and entrepreneur. She lives on the East Coast with her multiracial, bi-faith family, raising two Jewish children of color ages six and two. Tabitha writes the biweekly column, Raising Anti-Racist Kids, and was one of the founding members of the Women's March.

She/Her	2 Kids	Woman	Black

TL;DR: Raising an anti-racist baby is about more than reading books about diversity and bringing your baby along to protests. Anti-racism is a learned behavior, which means their education on equality starts with the everyday choices you make about your community.

As parents of a multiracial family, my partner and I wanted to raise anti-racist babies. To us, an anti-racist baby is one whose orientation and manifestation in this world rejects racism and centers equity and justice for all. This is evident through your parenting practices and the values and actions that provide the framework for how the family shows up in society. When our son was born, we assumed we had some time to figure things out, but we soon learned we were wrong.

Babies learn and observe a lot right from birth. Our son was taking in so much that by the time he was a toddler, he had already tried to identify his own race. Research shows that three-month-old babies prefer faces from certain racial groups, and nine-month-olds tend to use race to categorize faces.[1] So it's important to start incorporating anti-racist practices into your parenting as early as possible, no matter what color your skin is.

Raising an anti-racist baby starts with being intentional about what you read, what you do, and the people you interact with to center your parenting on justice and equity. By the time our second baby came along, my partner and I committed to three anti-racist pathways.

Education
Building an anti-racist library for our babies was a fun part of educating them. We stock their bookshelves with diverse authors and protagonists of color. It's important to learn about histories like Rosa Parks, Martin Luther King Jr., and the Civil Rights Movement, but it was also key for our babies to see narratives with kids and people of color just existing and finding joy.

Practice
We moved what we taught into action as a family—we took our baby to marches and peaceful protests. Our daughter was one month old at her first march in Washington, DC. We bundled her up in her stroller, pumped some extra breastmilk for the journey, and off we went. We didn't underestimate what our baby was taking in around her.

Community
We were intentional about the people our baby interacted with and how she saw us interact with others. Our community includes friends, family, caregivers, and people in our neighborhood.

Making anti-racist practices the family norm is key to raising babies in a society centered on justice and equity. It is within our power to create a society where all kids have opportunities to thrive, and it starts with what you do at home.

HELPFUL TIPS:

Set realistic goals for yourself. For example, read one book every day to your baby, or with your child present, do one community activity a month that focuses on anti-racist education.

Look for books written and illustrated by people of color that also have protagonists of color. It's key for children of color to see themselves reflected in the media they consume. It's also important for white children to see protagonists of color as active participants in the world we envision.

Social media is a great place to find musicians of color who specialize in music for babies. The diversity of who we are is reflected in how we sound too. Adding a rich diversity of voices to your world builds comfort with and respect for hearing those voices throughout your life.

Examine where you get your parenting advice. Social media is a great place to build community online, and many groups are for parents from diverse backgrounds. If you're white and only a part of groups with other white parents, your perspective will be limited and you can miss vital information about anti-racist parenting practices.

[1]Jess Sullivan, Leigh Solano Wilton, and Evan Apfelbaum, "Adults Delay Conversations about Race Because They Underestimate Children's Processing of Race," *Journal of Experimental Psychology: General*, 2020, https://doi.org/10.31234/osf.io/5xpsa.

"Raising an anti-racist baby starts with being intentional about what you read, what you do, and the people you interact with to center your parenting on justice and equity."

Chapter 2

LETTING THEM PAVE THE WAY.

When to let them learn the hard way.

Orly Agai Marley is an entrepreneur, manager, wife, and mother. She was born in Israel, has lived in California for most of her life, is married to Ziggy Marley (eldest son of legendary musician, Bob Marley), and has four children. Orly and Ziggy have built a record label, Tuff Gong Worldwide, a music publishing company, Ishti Music, and a nonprofit, Unlimited Resources Giving Enlightenment (U.R.G.E.), which seeks to make enduring contributions to the lives of children in Jamaica and around the world by supporting their educational, health, and environmental needs.

She/Her	4 Kids	Heterosexual	Middle Eastern

TL;DR: Surround your child with love and support, but let them make their own way forward.

A wise woman once told me, "A parent is only as happy as their least happy child." At the time, my children were young, and their obstacles were minimal. Now a parent to seventeen-, fifteen-, eleven-, and six-year-old children, I am able to reflect on those words with greater depth and understanding.

The truth of the matter is, as your children grow, so do the obstacles the world presents them with—leaving us as parents to wonder whether we should help pave the road for them, or give them the space to pave their own path.

As an immigrant who came to America at the age of fourteen, I was met with an unfamiliar world and was forced to navigate the ins and outs of American culture on my own.

My parents were not in a position to physically, mentally, or financially guide me the way most American parents did. Additionally, as the first-born child, I was expected to support, guide, and monitor my two younger siblings, who were nine and ten years younger than me.

Although I was resentful, I am now grateful this was my reality. I persevered and worked hard throughout my life, knowing there was no silver platter or spoon. I think about my children and their world today and continuously try to keep my helicoptering tendencies in check so they can create their own experiences and learn from their own mistakes.

I know their challenges will not be my own, as they were born into a more economically and financially stable environment. They will have their own struggles and triumphs. These will be their own. *Their* own to navigate. *Their* own to conquer. *Their* own to fail.

Ultimately, for us as parents, we need to keep an even keel, stay calm, and make sure our own figurative cupboards are full.

Emphasize nourishing and nurturing your soul so you can give back to your children. If your cupboard is full, you are then able to dispense and give love and attention to your children.

So, fill up your souls, parents, and carry on.

"I think about my children and their world today and continuously try to keep my helicoptering tendencies in check so they can create their own experiences and learn from their own mistakes."

Chapter 3

MISINFORMATION.

Being online does not equal being qualified.

Dr. Mona Amin is a board-certified general pediatrician and mother. She is on social media as @PedsDocTalk, sharing educational and motivational information to remind parents they are doing an amazing job raising their children.

1 Kid	Married	Indian American

TL;DR: There's plenty of useful information on the internet, but it can also be overwhelming, contradictory, and heavily based on opinion. Find a set of credible sources to avoid making misinformed decisions.

As modern parents, we are lucky to have access to the knowledge of our inner circle as well as information on the internet. It can feel like we hit the jackpot! Unsure of what to do when your child has a cold? Look it up online! Unsure of how to manage a tantrum? Look it up online! Unsure about vaccines for your child? Look it up online!

But wait… The internet is great for so many things, but as a pediatrician, mom, and social media educator, I know how fast misinformation spreads online and how it negatively affects parents. We can feel overwhelmed by the amount of contradictory information out there, which can lead to making misinformed decisions.

On social media, there are so many different opinions on various topics: parenting, health, and the safety of our children, to name a few. But, unfortunately, anyone can create a profile or blog, and not all of them will provide correct information.

Misinformation.

So, how do parents decipher valid information and misinfor-mation?

The first thing you can do is look at the credentials of the people providing the information. Are they licensed to discuss the topic from a nationally or internationally recognized licensing board? Are they giving information that is in their scope of practice?

You wouldn't call a lawyer to fix a broken pipe—you would hire a plumber. So why take advice on vaccines from someone who doesn't administer them or take care of infectious diseases?

The next thing parents can examine is whether what they find online largely contradicts what they hear elsewhere. We are all entitled to have various opinions, but when it comes to the health and safety of our babies and children, think of the material being given to you in more detail.

- Does the person explain their thought process when discussing potentially divisive topics?
- Does the person have evidence to back up their claims?
- Does the person criticize others to make a point?

Even within certain niches, like feeding, sleep, and develop-ment, there is contradictory information because so much of what we know is based on opinion and not evidence.

The goal is to follow a small set of accounts that give credible, reliable information from relevant experts who have support to back up their claims.

We all have a right to be educated and the internet is a great resource, but it requires a little work on your part to filter out the noise and make sure you consume sound information.

Chapter 4

BUILDING PARENTING SKILLS.

Give love to yourself so you have more love to give.

Jessi Duley is a creator, a mother, an encourager, a founder, a risk-taker, a lunch maker, a list maker, a day maker, and a troublemaker. Her favorite color is checkered (like her past), and she says, "Actually, I can," to herself a lot. Jessi is an entrepreneur who started and grew her health and fitness business, BurnCycle, at the exact same time she started and grew her family. She doesn't think she started out good at either and has stumbled and bumbled her way through entrepreneurship and motherhood. In conclusion, she believes if you can be kind to yourself, you can do all the hard things. And snacks always help.

She/Her	3 Kids	Married

TL;DR: Build the skills you need as a parent the same as you would for any job or goal you set. The work of parenting is the most important work out there, and the love, grace, and ingenuity you show up with will help shape your child in invaluable ways—even when we don't do it perfectly.

My daughter was born fourteen days before the launch of my first business. Every idea of what I thought motherhood was would be reshaped, recreated, and humbled by the messy and beautiful reality of those first three months.

As a "high-functioning" professional woman, I thought I could handle it, just like the women I saw and read about on the internet. I couldn't, and I realized that's okay. Because if I didn't give myself grace and compassion as a new mother, how could I give it to my child and raise them with love?

There will be times when you feel overwhelmed, underqualified, overextended, and underwater—and that's okay because to build your strength, you need to wear your heart on the outside.

There will be times when you feel like a failure—and that's okay too. You've never done this before, and when your child experiences failure, you will know what to say.

There will be times when you will take an hour by yourself over any time with friends—and that's okay. You deserve it, and you will teach your child the importance of self-care and boundaries.

There will be times when you compare yourself to other parents and criticize yourself—and that's okay. It's natural, but deep down we all know each journey into parenthood is our own, and recognizing that will help you create a home of acceptance and compassion.

There will be times you feel like you're screaming on the inside because you can't communicate with a screaming baby—and that's okay. It will pass, and the patience you develop early on will help you hold space for the big feelings our little ones have as they grow.

There will be times when you're covered in bodily fluids—any combination of baby barf, baby poop, and possibly your own tears—and it's okay to leave the house like that. You're surviving and doing the best you can.

There will come a time when you realize that dream of all natural wooden toys is gone and your house is full of plastic—and that's okay. A loving and functional house is a house that is real, and real is always better.

The Big Picture.

There will be times you wonder if you will ever feel connected to your partner again—and you will. And your child will see that prioritizing connection and friendship is where the foundation of love and respect comes from.

There will be times when you feel guilty because you are excited to leave for work. Because you feel more fulfilled from work than you do from parenting—and that's okay. You're better at it, you've been doing it longer than you've been parenting, and when it's time to show your kids the importance of practice and not giving up, you will have already led by example and have the lived experience with which to teach them.

There will be times when nothing goes as planned, and everything goes sideways, and it will happen again, and again, and again—and that's okay. Because that's the beauty of life, and you will raise a child who can bounce back and roll with the punches.

There will be times when you can't believe the love you feel for your baby, your child, your legacy of a lifetime—and in those moments pause, and just be. Let it wash over you and fill you up because to feel a depth of love from a parent to a child is one of the greatest gifts of our lifetime. And know that this unconditional love, the love your baby feels, *that* love will change the world.

"Because if I didn't give myself grace and compassion as a new mother, how could I give it to my child and raise them with love?"

Chapter 5

GENDER EXPECTATIONS.

Congratulations, they're a human!

Noleca Anderson Radway is the founder of Quarks, a production company that specializes in audio and visual art through a Black Queer lens. Noleca is a Bronx-raised, first-generation Black-Jamaican, wife, mother, educator, and Octavia Butler fan. She is the producer and host of the progressive parenting podcast *Raising Rebels*. Noleca graduated from Howard University and attended Bank Street College of Education. She lives in Amsterdam, Netherlands, with her partner and their three children.

She/They	3 Kids	Queer	Jamaican

TL;DR: We live in a world shaped by harmful gender stereotypes, and those stereotypes start very early. Advocating for your little one means learning new language and tossing out old expectations.

As a progressive educator, I was well-versed in the negative effects of gender norms on children long before I became pregnant with my first child. So, when it was my turn, I decided to do everything I could think of to keep gender socialization at bay.

I made it clear to my OBGYN that I did not want to know the sex of my baby. I searched for names that would counter a limited narrative. If we had a girl, we would give her my father's name, and if we had a boy, we would name him after my partner's mother. We painted our nursery apple green and made sure to buy pink trucks and blue teddy bears.

And then, on a cold January day, our baby was born, and we named her Blu.

Gender Expectations.

The first question everyone asked was, "Boy or girl?"

I enthusiastically answered, "She's a girl!"

All of my righteous objections to our gendered society went right out the window. Instead, I welcomed the parade of pink. Gendering our baby gave me language and a way to relate to her and my community. I immediately thought I understood things about this little person just because I identified her as a girl. But, it is detrimental to think you know a person before they know themselves—or before anyone can truly know them.

You stop being curious right when there is so much to learn.

There are better, more interesting answers to "Boy or a girl?". Answers that challenge heteronomative thinking and make adults uncomfortable in the best ways. Answers like, "I don't know the gender of my child and they were born with a penis."

Too often, people say something well-meaning, but actually quite sexist.

"He is such a good boy."
"She is such a sweet girl."
"That boy energy is a lot."
"She is such a flirt already!"

These statements are harmful and begin to create boxes for our children. So, call them out every time.

"They are not good or bad, they are just being."
"We don't value sweetness."
"I love their energy! It is so powerful."
"Please don't sexualize my baby."

Unaware adults might ask you to become co-conspirators in the oppression of your children (yes, it's oppression). So be mindful, be vigilant, and lead with love.

Chapter 6

HOW VACCINES WORK.

A parable about narwhals and vaccines.

Dr. Malia Jones, PhD, is a scientist, maker, partner, and mom of two boys, ages seven and eleven. She is an associate scientist at the University of Wisconsin-Madison, where she studies infectious disease epidemiology. She earned a master's and doctorate in public health from UCLA and completed postdoctoral training in preventive medicine at the University of Southern California. In other words, she lives in Wisconsin and studies how people think about vaccines.

She/They	2 Kids	Heterosexual	White

TL;DR: Very early in your parenting journey, you'll come across the topic of vaccines and will need to make some big decisions. Deciding to get you and your child vaccinated is an investment in the health of you, your family, and your community.

Imagine you woke up tomorrow morning and there was a narwhal lounging in your bathtub.

You've probably never seen a real narwhal before. Nonetheless, you'd know what it was. You've seen pictures of narwhals before, so you know the special patterns, shapes, and features of narwhals. (If you haven't seen a picture of a narwhal, go ahead and Google it right now. I'll wait.)

A picture of a narwhal is completely harmless. But a real narwhal in your tub would be a big problem that you'd want to do something about right away.

How Vaccines Work.

That's how a vaccine works. The active ingredients in a vaccine show your immune system a harmless model of something that makes you sick—a virus or other pathogen.

There are several ways to create these models. Some vaccines use weak or dead versions of the pathogen. Others use little pieces of them, and still other vaccines just contain a blueprint for your own cells to make little pieces of the pathogen for a short time.

But no matter which type of vaccine you get, what happens next is always the same: your own fantastic, natural immune system memorizes the special patterns, shapes, and features it sees in the model and tucks them away for future reference.

Later, if you encounter "the real narwhal," your immune cells recognize that it's a threat right away and take speedy action to protect you. Some vaccines take more than one dose, which is a little bit like seeing several pictures of narwhals from different angles.

Our immune systems are amazing. They are incredibly complex and perfectly adapted to the process of identifying and memorizing things that might make us sick.

Vaccines are a low-risk way to capitalize on your natural ability to fight off infections. And when your immune system prevents an infection before it begins, it also keeps you from infecting anyone else. That means vaccines protect both you and the people around you.

At some point in your parenting journey, you'll come across stories about vaccine injuries. These stories are frightening. When we are frightened, we don't think rationally, and we tend to ignore the big picture.

In truth, the risks associated with vaccines are vanishingly small. In every single case, your child's risk from the infectious disease itself is bigger than the threat posed by the vaccine.

As always, talk to your pediatrician if you've got questions, concerns, or want to know more.

Here's the big picture: I got my kids vaccinated—and I am vaccinated—because I want to protect my children and the people we love. Even if I could be sure my kids would be just fine if they got sick, I'd still get them vaccinated because I don't want to put anyone else at risk.

Vaccination isn't just for you. It's for everyone. Vaccines are all about community. The goal is to keep *everyone* safe from infectious diseases.

Definitions

Vaccine: A medication that stimulates a person's immune system, protecting them from a specific disease.

Vaccinate: to administer a vaccine, usually by injection.

Pathogen: a tiny organism (like a virus or bacterium) that can make you sick.

Narwhal: an arctic whale which, in the male, possesses one or (rarely) two long, spiraling tusks.

Virus: an infectious agent capable of growth and multiplication in the body and which causes disease and sickness.

Infectious disease: a disease caused by microorganisms such as viruses.

Immune system: the organs and processes in the body which protect from illness and infection.

Active ingredient: the part of a substance or compound which produces its biological or chemical effect.

"The active ingredients in a vaccine show your immune system a harmless model of something that makes you sick—a virus or other pathogen."

Chapter 7

SENSE OF PURPOSE.

Taking on life's greatest responsibility.

Emmitt Smith is a professional football icon, businessman, and entrepreneur. One of the greatest to play the game, Smith competed for 15 seasons in the NFL, complete with three Super Bowl rings and eight Pro Bowl honors. In 2010, the Pensacola, Florida, native was inducted into the Pro Football Hall of Fame and selected for the NFL 100 All-Time Team in 2019. Smith now resides in Dallas where he runs several successful businesses and is active in local and national charitable outreach. Above all his athletic accomplishments and business efforts, Smith's greatest honor and joy is being a father to his five children.

5 Kids	Black

TL;DR: Regardless of how prepared you feel, when your baby comes into this world, they become your main priority and everything you do is about caring and providing for them. Books, classes, and others' advice will help, but parenting is mostly firsthand experience, so just do your best!

There is no combination of words that appropriately describe your emotions when you hold your child for the first time. Everything becomes about them—your entire world. You become overwhelmed with a sense of purpose, knowing you have discovered your life's greatest responsibility.

Now, let me tell you...the first night home from the hospital is nerve-wracking. No one tells you everything you're supposed to do, and there's certainly no manual for this either. There will also come a point where you realize just how much the nurses at the hospital were doing to help you!

We hovered over each of our baby's cribs all night long, but once you make it through the first night, every night after becomes a little bit easier. The thing about being a parent is, that sense of worry never fully goes away no matter how old your children get. You learn to manage it better, but it's just part of being a loving and protective parent.

Almost all your parenting skills will come through experience. You try to draw from lessons your parents taught you, books you've read, what you researched online, and maybe even from professionals who've offered advice. You do your best, you have open conversations with your partner, but at the end of the day, it's all experience, and you adjust as you go.

In that first year, I recommend asking for help from your own parents, if that's an option for you. They've been in your position before and know to a certain extent what you might be going through. Having a baby is a huge change in your life, so being able to rely on your parents, not just as a support system for your child but also for you, is a huge blessing.

My final words of advice to first-time parents would be to enjoy every moment. Time will fly by, and before you know it, you will long for those first moments. So, be present and enjoy it all, because it's one of the best gifts in this life.

"The thing about being a parent is, that sense of worry never fully goes away no matter how old your children get."

Chapter 8

RAISING A MIXED-RACE CHILD.

Affirming your child's identity so they can be all of who they are.

Dr. Jennifer Noble, PhD, is a parent coach, child psychologist, and advocate for the mixed-race community. She is of African American and Sri Lankan Tamil descent, a California native who has traveled to over thirty-five countries, and loves anything with coconut. She is a Super Auntie to nieces and nephews all over the globe who enjoy going on adventures and sharing their lives with her.

She/Her	Cisgender	Tamil Sri Lankan	African American

TL;DR: Raising a mixed-race kid means arming yourself with information and being prepared to respond to awkward questions. Most importantly, it means celebrating the uniqueness of your child's identity.

So, your new baby is mixed race. They now join over nine million people who are mixed race in the United States alone.

Your baby's life experience will be unique and possibly totally different from yours. Mixed-race people often feel like they don't belong—that they're not enough. Our society doesn't yet fully understand the mixed-race experience (Madame VP Kamala Harris knows).

You might be thinking, "Not my little one. They'll be confident and proud of their unique heritage. Just tell me what we need to do!" No problem!

Speak Up. People will say things—hurtful and ridiculous things—to you and your kid. So, speak up and affirm your baby until they can speak up for themselves.

Practice your firm replies, snark, and sarcasm.

"My kid is both ___ and ___. They don't need to choose."
"Am I their dad? Why? Are you with *The Maury Povich Show*?"
"No, I'm not the nanny, but we're looking for one."

It can be scary to speak up, and even more challenging to speak up to family and teachers. But you will need to, and I know you can!

Cultural Exposure. Iris Apfel, a one-hundred-year-old fashionista, says, "More is more." She's right—especially for cultural exposure.

Think about the ways you can expose your kiddo to language, food, music, holidays, religious traditions, festivals, art, dance, traditional dress, and more. The more they experience the richness of their cultures, the more they'll feel a part of it. Involving extended family is an excellent way to do this, and if you can travel to a faraway homeland, even better.

Consider Community. Is your community racially and ethnically diverse? Do you have friends with mixed-race kids? Will your kid be the only one who looks like them at school? Are you far from extended family? Can you join an ethnic community?

Belonging and acceptance are super important. It's up to you to provide a community where developing both is possible.

I know this feels like a lot, but it just requires intentionality. As their loving parent, you're already equipped to affirm your mixed-race child.

"Your baby's life experience will be unique and possibly totally different from yours."

Chapter 9

PRESENT VS. FUTURE NEEDS.

Budgeting for a baby doesn't have to break the bank.

LaToia Levy Johnson is a native of Pittsburg, California, and a single Black mother of two sons ages twenty-one and three. She is a mortgage underwriter, writer, and poet.

She/Her	2 Kids	Divorced	African American

TL;DR: Avoid the temptation to overspend on your new little one and focus on long-term needs, just-in-case must-haves, and practical support.

I was awarded the title of Mommy when I was nineteen.

Enraptured by the thought of a brand-new baby, I shopped for cute clothes, toys, and things to decorate the tiny space he would occupy in our one-bedroom apartment. I assumed the baby shower gifts would cover the rest of the essentials. I was wrong.

I soon realized how financially ill-prepared I was for parenthood, especially as the costs of returning to work trickled in and things like formula and childcare became necessary expenses.

My evolution to motherhood with my first son revealed life lessons I implemented with my second, almost twenty years later. With babies come expected and unexpected necessities, and these are a few gems I learned about budgeting for baby.

Savings will be your bestie.
Instead of splurging on clothes your baby may only wear once,

shop sales and research coupons and other discounts before making purchases. Resell the excess to fund needed items.

Price out priorities first.
For your child's first year, some of your priority needs will be diapers in multiple sizes, a car seat, stroller, crib and crib sheet, formula (price it whether you think you'll need it or not), and a suitable breast pump, if you're breastfeeding.

Plan for the life you want.
Consider whether you're going to be a stay-at-home parent or if your child will attend daycare. With both comes serious vetting to understand costs. Envision the life you want for your child when considering your budget.

Don't forget about freebies.
Search online for "freebies for new parents" to connect with companies offering free diapers, formula, clothing, and more.

Do your research.
Research local government programs as well as religious or social organizations that assist families in need. Grants and financial assistance may be available for diapers and food items.

Join groups that share resources.
Parenting groups can be a great source of savings by sharing out-grown clothing, overbought items, or simple money-saving best practices. They're also a great way to find community.

Tap into your tribe.
Remember, you're not the only one excited about this beautiful addition to your life. Others await the opportunity to contribute, so tug on your tribe as needed. Don't feel like you're failing because you want (and need) help.

These are just a few tips, but know you will figure things out as you determine your own plan. Don't panic. You've got this!

You can do this!

Chapter 10

ATTACHMENT PARENTING.

Follow your instincts—there isn't one "right" way to be a parent.

Evelyn Yang is an advocate, author, and proud parent of two boys with special needs. She is a foodie, a universal basic income zealot, and a native New Yorker who is often mistaken for a Californian.

She/Her	2 Kids	Married	AAPI

TL;DR: Learn to tap into your instincts as a new parent by believing you're the world's leading expert on your own baby.

"The more people have studied different methods of bringing up children, the more they have come to the conclusion that what good mothers and fathers instinctively feel like doing for their babies is usually best after all." —Dr. Benjamin Spock

Dr. Spock was an American pediatrician with a ground-breaking and best-selling parenting book first published in 1946. A lot has changed since then, but fundamental human instincts have not. As the mother of two boys, six and nine, I'm just now getting out of the weeds. I'm not going to lie—the first few years aren't easy. It was more work than I ever anticipated. But trusting my instincts every step of the way has kept me feeling positive overall and confident that I've been a good (and, at times, even great) mother.

I follow a method known as attachment parenting, first popularized by pediatrician and best-selling author, Dr. William

Sears—the father of 8 children and author of over 40 books on childcare. People have tried to break this down into a to-do list that includes things like breastfeeding and baby-wearing. To me, you don't need a checklist—attachment parenting basically means being sensitive and responsive to your baby's needs. In other words, trust that your baby, and your relationship with your baby, will guide what you need to do.

What seems to make your baby happy? What gives your baby comfort? What do you feel good doing? Humans have been childbearing and childrearing for a long time—well before parenting books. These days we get so hung up on certain rules, whether from parenting books or advice from well-meaning friends and family members who swear by their own experiences.

In my case, my son had autism, which can be hard to diagnose before age four. He had different sensory needs. He couldn't sleep unless his skin was touching mine. I struggled for a while trying to have him sleep alone before I gave in to my own instincts and did what made both of us happy. I have no doubt now that the cry-it-out method would have never worked, despite how long I tried, despite how well I know it works for some babies. But it was impossible to know then that my son had different needs, so I am so glad I went with what felt right at the time.

Don't be afraid to trust your instincts. Trust that you are programmed to be a nurturer and that you know what you're doing. This is also why people say the second kid is so much easier. By then, you've figured out that all the rules are mostly extraneous. Your baby will be just fine, and you are all they need. Since you're reading this book, I have a feeling you are already ahead.

"...trust that your baby, and your relationship with your baby, will guide you in what you need to do."

Chapter 11

DAY-TO-DAY FEARS.

A little perspective goes a long way.

Gearah Goldstein is the mother of two wonderful kids. She forms her reflections around the unique experience of raising her kids while also identifying as transgender. She and her wife have been married for twenty-nine years.

She/Her	Married	Transgender	Jewish

TL;DR: Set aside the worry and fear of new parenthood. Meet your challenging moments with a deep breath and a little grace.

Regardless of how well prepared you are to welcome your first baby into your life, you will sometimes find yourself feeling overwhelmed, and that's okay. There is so much to learn, so much to do. You will likely feel new pressures from your family and friends. You will probably sense your family is also feeling the pressures of all the changes happening around them.

People will offer you suggestions about *everything*. They will bombard you with information and "helpful tips" you never requested. The list of pressures and changes can go on and on for pages, but I hope the following words will help you keep things in perspective. Then, in the future, when you are feeling overwhelmed, I hope you'll revisit this page and find some comfort.

Remember that human beings have been raising babies since the beginning of human beings. It is part of our DNA, part of our instinctual behavior, part of the beauty of the universe. Nature has uniquely equipped you to raise babies. If you're reading this book, particularly this chapter, I can assume you're looking for some tips to calm your worries. Here are some of mine.

Breathe.
Find moments to focus on breathing. Inhale slowly through your nose for four seconds...and exhale through your mouth for four seconds. While breathing in, think about kindness and calmness. When breathing out, think about putting down something too heavy to carry.

Practice gratitude and empathy.
Ask yourself, "What am I grateful for?" Once you answer that question, ask it again. Keep answering and repeat until you count five things. Then, offer yourself the same empathy you would offer your baby. Give yourself the space to be okay with feeling overwhelmed.

Take in each moment.
Nothing is forever. Try to focus on the moment while understanding that the moment will pass. If the moment is wonderful, cherish it, love it, feel the warmth in it. If the moment is awful, recognize that it will end and you will find wonderful moments again.

Raising a child is not easy. It's not supposed to be. Through this experience, you will learn more about yourself than ever before. You will become stronger with each setback and each triumph, and you will grow with your child.

You've got this! Understand that you are not alone. For everything you feel and experience as a new parent, countless families have been through similar. Before you know it, like me, you'll be reaching back to help other new parents with their children. And, like me, you'll be shocked by how quickly the lessons come. It's not until you share your knowledge that you recognize how much you have learned.

Enjoy it all!

Chapter 12

LIVING WITH YOUR PARENT.

On mothering while being mothered.

Rachael Lucille Van Klompenberg is a Portland-area native, raising her kids to be inclusive leaders, friends, and advocates. Her personal and professional focuses are relationship-building, elevating the voices of those often overlooked, and challenging the status quo to create a more inclusive world. In her spare time you'll catch her sharing her life via Instagram, reading sci-fi young adult novels, skateboarding, or lounging near water.

She/Her	3 Kids	Queer	Black

TL;DR: Being a parent means having the lifelong joy of being a sanctuary for your kids whenever they need help, comfort, or wisdom.

When my son, Jett, was born, I was only twenty-two years old. Though I had checked off many of the traditional adulting items from my list (Graduate from high school—CHECK. Get a college degree—CHECK. Get a stable job in my field—CHECK.), I was naïve, and to some degree didn't actually feel like an adult. I lived very comfortably at home with my mom, who still found joy in mothering me.

My mom made it clear the moment Jett and I returned home from the hospital that her job as a mother wasn't over. In fact, it now extended to her new grandbaby. After a cesarean section birth, I had lovingly strict instructions to sleep when baby slept and to focus as much on the bond between me and Jett as possible. My mom walked alongside me every step of the way, from teary-eyed, sleepless nights to the many Saturday mornings she'd wake up with Jett so I could sleep in. At the time, it felt like too much fuss, but after my second postpartum experience, I realized that my mom gave me the hands-on support and advice every new parent needs but many don't receive.

As a new mom who was often labeled as too young, inexperienced, and sheltered to excel at parenting, I felt pressure to exceed everyone's expectations. I read up on childhood development, memorized the milestones, made the ambitious goal of extended breastfeeding, and—against my mother's advice—immediately tried to repurpose nap times as opportunities to fulfill domestic duties. I was a mom now and I needed to act like it. But it didn't take long for me to burn out, and in those moments, my mother reminded me she was there to support me, and her job as mother to me was not over.

Actively being mothered as a new mom taught me more than I could've ever learned Googling "childhood development." Being a mother isn't just about milestones, cooking, or driving a minivan. And being a mother doesn't end when our kids become "adults."

My mom taught me that being a mother is being a sanctuary. It's holding our kids when they're exhausted, listening to their thoughts without judgment or shame, and encouraging them to experience the wide range of feelings we're all born with—no matter how old we are.

Being a mother means giving your kid the confidence to make their dreams come true and admitting there's no such thing as perfection.

Being a mother is a lifelong joy that we may eventually be fortunate enough to share with our own kids.

Chapter 13

TWO WORLDVIEWS.

Managing divergent cultures within one home.

David Kim is a Korean American dad raising two girls, Skylar and Zoey, and is married to Nina, who is also Korean American. He lives in Silicon Valley and is a pastor and author of *A Kids Book About Change*.

He/Him	2 Kids	Married	Asian American

TL;DR: Navigating different cultural perspectives when raising your children can feel overwhelming. What matters is honing in on the aspects of each culture that fit your family best.

"You are going to speak Korean to Skylar at home, right?"
"The best thing is for you to work and for Nina to stay home."
"You should sleep train by letting the baby cry it out."

Skylar is three months old, and honestly, all I'm trying to do is find diapers that are on sale and make sure she is healthy.

As soon as a child enters your life, everyone has something to say. From family and friends to media and culture, there are both spoken and unspoken expectations for what successful parenting looks like. As a Korean American bicultural dad, I'm carrying both the expectations and values of my Asian, immigrant culture as well as the Western, Silicon Valley culture I grew up with.

The West values individual choice and freedom:
"Try new ways of doing things."
"You must be the very best."
"Put yourself first."

Two Worldviews.

The East values tradition and community:
    "This is how we've always done it."
    "You must not be an embarrassment."
    "Put your community first."

To me, both Eastern and Western cultures have good points, and I find myself living within that tension. There are beautiful aspects worth celebrating, and unnecessary aspects, which are exhausting to live up to and must be acknowledged.

I have found two things to be really helpful in navigating both cultures in our family: preservation and integration.

Preservation: Talk about values which are important that you want to preserve in your family.

Integration: Find ways to integrate those values in the rhythms of your family.

For our family, this looks like honoring one another's individual preferences and giving space to freely express our needs and wants while also sharing the stories and importance of our past, eating amazing Korean food, and speaking Korean to our kids.

For example, every new year our family gathers together with relatives to eat a traditional rice cake soup, pay respects to our elders, and receive new year blessings from them. We value wisdom and honoring those who are further along on the journey of life.

Without both preservation and integration, confusion and misunderstandings about expectations can happen easily. Finding what worked best for our family was crucial to maintain harmony.

I used to think carrying two cultures was a burden. But it's actually a blessing.

"From family and friends to media and culture, there are both spoken and unspoken expectations for what successful parenting looks like."

Chapter 14

WHEN YOUR CHILD IS REALLY SICK.

How to face the unplannable.

Jen (she/her) and **Ruben** (he/him) **Alvarado** live in the Pacific Northwest with their fifteen-year-old son. As a family, the Alvarados enjoy board games, swimming, and playing with their sweet family dog, Macks.

Married	1 kid	Jen: White	Ruben: Biracial

TL;DR: Making a plan is a good way to find security. But parenting requires flexibility. Embrace a plan that changes with you.

Prospective parents are all about planning. We create the perfect birth plan, dream of the moment we first meet our child, and pick out the cutest outfit for them to wear home. We anticipate blissful months spent bonding at home and design the ideal nursery.

We can't wait to document the first-year milestones in an Instagram-worthy way. We read all of the parenting books to figure out exactly which method will ensure our child is well-adjusted, sleeps well, and has the perfect childhood. All of this planning can build confidence in new parents. Our new adventure is beginning and we're ready for it!

Our parenting journey taught us that no one tells you how to plan for the unplannable, things like delays in milestones, having a sick child, family drama, breastfeeding complications, sleeping difficulties, or your own emotional responses to change. The first twelve months with our son were spent in and out of hospitals, taking ambulance rides, missing early milestones, and staying at a Ronald McDonald House.

In so many of those hard places, we found something we didn't anticipate: we were not alone, but rather surrounded by a beautiful community of other parents facing the unplannable. We discovered the beauty in strangers becoming instant friends and receiving wisdom from those who had been in these spaces even longer than we had.

This unanticipated community taught us to let go and embrace the unexpected. We learned that successful parenting is less about the perfect experience or achieving milestones and more about facing each thing as it comes, realizing the beauty in places where you didn't expect to find yourself.

Parents, it is so important to plan. Planning helps us feel equipped and prepared. So go ahead and make the plan, pursue the plan, and love the plan. Just remember, sometimes you have to let go of the plan. There is no guilt in that. Learning to release that shame lets you embrace the beauty of adjusting to this new life and all of its uniqueness.

"We learned that successful parenting is less about the perfect experience or achieving milestones and more about facing each thing as it comes, realizing the beauty in places where you didn't expect to find yourself."

Chapter 15

LEARNING ALONGSIDE YOUR CHILD.

Learning and relearning while parenting.

Denise Woodard is mom to Vivienne (7) and wife to Jeremy and lives in New York City. She's the founder/CEO of Partake Foods, a line of allergy-friendly foods inspired by Vivienne's experience with food allergies.

She/Her	1 Kid	Married	Black/Korean

TL;DR: No parent knows exactly how to be a parent before their baby arrives. Instead of trying to have it all figured out, develop a lens on parenting that is growth-oriented, for both you and your child. As new challenges come and go, you and your baby will grow and learn together.

Did you know that snails are born without shells? As they grow, so do their shells.

I'm including snail trivia in a parenting book because what I've learned is the concept of "figuring it all out" is a big myth.

No one has it all figured out when it comes to parenting, and that's part of the gift—as you teach your child, you also get the opportunity to learn more about yourself, growing together a bit each day. And like a tiny little snail, over time your parenting shell will get bigger.

I grew up an only child with no extended family nearby. There were no babies in my life. When I learned I was pregnant with Vivienne, I was excited, so happy, and really, really nervous.

How could I, someone who had never changed a diaper or held a baby, be responsible for another human life? I took every class known to man—Baby Care 101, CPR, even a singing class, because I was so convinced my lullaby singing would scar her. (I wish I was exaggerating, but I'm not.)

And then Vivi arrived. And I was still scared, but over time, I got so comfortable and confident in the parenting skills I needed in that moment—until the next big thing happened.

In Vivienne's first year, a big challenge we navigated was understanding her colic and realizing that it was the first presentation of her food allergies. We relied on different social media communities and doctors for help, as well as the help from my mother, mother-in-law, and trusted professionals.

Whether it was learning she had food allergies, the multiple sleep regressions, or the bigger conversations that have happened as she's gotten older, my shell has gotten bigger as we've both grown together.

The longer I'm a parent, the more I am reminded that things don't get easier. But, over time, I grow more confident and more resilient.

Find moments to remind yourself that your shell is growing, too.

"No one has it all figured out when it comes to parenting, and that's part of the gift—as you teach your child, you also get the opportunity to learn more about yourself as a parent, growing together a bit each day."

Chapter 16

HUMOR.

Choosing humor as a parenting philosophy.

Elizabeth Stock lives in Portland, Oregon, with her husband and two kids, Westley and Max. She balances parenthood with her day job leading a community organization with the mission of building a better tech industry by ensuring people of all backgrounds are a part of it. If she's not working or hanging out with the kids, she's probably taking a nap. Because, parenthood.

She/Her	2 Kids	Married	White

TL;DR: Being a new parent means having not nearly enough sleep to provide for someone who needs constant attention and care, and that can feel really overwhelming. When you're in the thick of new parenthood and feeling drained, choose humor over fixation on the challenges, and introduce some levity and laughter to the day-to-day.

Okay, you're reading this because you're in the thick of it right now and might need a laugh.

It's very possible you haven't showered in days, you're running on very little sleep, and there's a pile of crusty dishes in the kitchen somewhere. Oh, and your baby just looked you right in the eye and pooped thirty seconds after you changed their latest poopy diaper. That same baby hasn't napped all day even though everything you read says they should only be awake for forty-five minutes at a time!

It's a lot right now. A lot, a lot.

It can be easy to feel defeated by it all. You might be thinking, Why isn't this going the way I thought it would? Is it me?

Let me assure you, it's not you. It's them!

This is what babies do. And if we spend too much time agonizing over the challenging things, we may miss out on seeing the entertaining and loveable things.

It's been helpful for me to choose humor as a parenting philosophy, especially during those low points. While there is definitely a benefit to letting ourselves cry and feel the depth of this transformative time in our lives, there is also (and, I believe, more) benefit in learning to keep some levity and laugh at it all.

I mean, the whole new baby thing is kind of hilarious. These tiny humans dictate our entire lives, and they are only a few days old! How silly is that?

And here's the good news: you're already sleep-deprived and delirious half the time, so might as well embrace the delirium and have a good time! Before you know it, your tiny babies will be giant humans who don't need a whole lot from you. Looking back on my first year of parenthood, I know I was overly focused on the mechanics of getting through the day instead of just enjoying the opportunity to laugh.

Let's be real. Getting pooped on is no fun at all, but it *is* pretty funny.

"These tiny babies dictate our entire lives, and they are only a few days old! How silly is that?"

Chapter 17

EXPECT THE UNEXPECTED.

Or, how experience can be our greatest teacher.

Kyle Steed is an artist, designer, and observer. Raised among the rolling hills of the humid US south, his work permeates space with color, shape, and balanced form. Kyle keeps busy by helping raise his two daughters with his wife, Amanda, in Dallas, Texas.

He/Him	2 Kids	Married

TL;DR: You can't plan for the surprises parenthood brings, but you can develop a mindset to expect the unexpected, which allows for greater flexibility and patience with yourself as a new parent.

The weeks and months flew by leading up to my first daughter's birth. My wife and I were given a due date of mid-December and she ended up coming three weeks early, at the end of November.

Expect the unexpected.

By the time my daughter was born, I was a full-time freelance designer and was booked for a job out of town. We went to see our midwife on a Thursday and were told we'd be having our baby that very next day. My plans—our life—were all about to change.

Expect the unexpected.

The day of her birth was one I thought would never end. I've never been witness to that amount of pain and joy all at once. And finally, when it came time for my wife to cross that threshold into motherhood, I was right there and would be the first person to welcome our daughter into the world.

Words failed me at this encounter with the divine.

Expect the unexpected.

Overcome with joy and a newfound sense of pride at being a father, it quickly dawned on me that now we were three. Driving home with our baby girl in the backseat was, and still is, one of the most surreal feelings in my life. This question of *What do we do now?* kept running through my mind.

If I were to offer any advice or encouragement it would be this: Learn how to pack snacks.

LOL! But it's so true. No matter where you are, or what you're doing, the kids will always love a good snack (and parents do too).

Also, learn how to be kind with yourself. Mistakes will be made, but they are one of life's greatest teachers. Kindness helps us learn from mistakes rather than regret them. And with a snack in your hand and a little love for yourself, there's nothing you can't face...including the unexpected.

"Mistakes will be made, but they are one of life's greatest teachers."

Chapter 18

MORAL RESPONSIBILITY.

Raising humans in an uncertain world.

Zola Ellen is an organizer and abolitionist living in Minneapolis, Minnesota. She is part of the Burn Something Collective, a 2020 Black Futures Lab Public Policy Institute fellow, writer, and visual storyteller. Zola is mama to the flyest preteen, Gabriel (12), and dog mama to a floppy Great Dane.

She/They	1 Kid	Queer	Black

TL;DR: In your baby's eyes, you see a world of hope. But on the news, things can seem dark and overwhelming. You can't dictate how the world will show up for your children, but you can influence how *they* will show up in the world.

I was round, cold, gassy, and pregnant during the time of year when the Minnesota air is so frigid it rushes to steal the heat from your breath. I was nineteen. As I tried to stay warm, I distracted myself by reading all about my favorite planet, the eighth from the sun, Neptune—gassy and cold, just like me. Meanwhile, my very own creature flailed around in my womb. I was becoming my own planet. His hands, knees, and elbows stretched out my belly as I said, "You are so you, my sweet alien."

My son was born in March, just a few months after Oscar Grant's last breath was stolen by Bay Area Rapid Transit (BART) police in Oakland, California. We only knew the truth because it was recorded, leaving a traumatizing video to circulate the internet.

By April, the first case of H1N1 (swine flu) was identified in the US. People died that year—at the hands of police and the grips of this virus. And then twelve years flew by.

"What advice would you give us?" my brother-in-law asked. We were sitting in a corner booth over a basket of fries in Minneapolis, a few blocks from 38th Street and Chicago Avenue. He was full of curiosity because he and my sister were expecting their first child. He wanted to know how they should feel, despite the chaos of the world, about welcoming a new, precious life into their family.

I wasn't sure what to say then, but here's what I say now to all the parents out there who are looking at the world, looking at their new baby, and starting to lose hope.

Write down what nourishes you.
This can be as simple as a favorite poem, a reminder to stand in the sun, or how good a perfectly ripe peach is. Have that list ready to reach for when life overwhelms you.

Be honest with yourself about yourself.
Our kids notice everything—literally. Even the lies. When we face ourselves, and forgive ourselves, our kids see generations of passed-down pain start to dissipate.

Unplug from the updates.
The world's weight will try to build a home in your mind and it can get so murky. Tell it *no*. Our minds belong to us, which means we sometimes have to take a break from doom scrolling. Put your phone down, or at least turn your notifications off.

Some days we'll yearn to be elsewhere, on a whole different planet. When you gaze at your child, remember you *are* the planet. A vessel of joy and grief; of knowledge and complexities; of ice cream; of resistance. A spinning rock reaching for the burning light of the sun—for an abundant world capable of keeping us all alive. Limitless.

Breathe in. Breathe out.

Chapter 19

OUR MONEY STORIES.

Discussing money early on will help set your child up for financial success in the future.

Georgia Lee Hussey is the founder and CEO of Modernist Financial, a wealth management firm in lovely Portland, Oregon, founded to help people structure their wealth around their progressive values. Before she became a certified financial planner, she made weird feminist performance art about labor and gender using molten glass, hot steel, and cast chocolate. She also wrote novels and short creative essays.

She/They	Child-Free	Queer	Femme

TL;DR: If you want your baby to grow up to have a grounded and emotionally balanced relationship with money, you need to talk about it. And it's never too early to start. Verbally processing financial decisions with your kids early on will help build architectures for financial decision-making which are explicit and practical and will set them up for the rest of their lives.

A money story is a narrative, often subconscious, that we tell ourselves about who and how we can be in relation to money. It's a storyline that unconsciously drives our many financial decisions, from today's grocery stop to the kind of work we think we can do.

I don't have children of my own, but I spend a lot of time helping adults do the tender work of discovering and rewriting the money stories they learned as kids.

Let's talk about money.

I've learned that adults who have the most grounded relationships with money usually grew up in families who talked about it—who openly discussed how much they earned, how much they worked, and how much the various elements of their lives cost. They understood why their family couldn't afford all the toys or luxuries. And they knew their inability to have everything they wanted was not a reflection of their worth or their parents' love, but the limitations we all navigate in our financial lives.

By verbally processing financial decisions within their families, kids build architectures for financial decision-making that are explicit and practical. Your little one isn't able to earn or spend money (yet!), but they'll get there one day. So, start preparing them now.

Let's broaden the definition of wealth.

Wealth can be what you have in the bank, but it's also the relationships you have within your community, the skills which help you thrive in life, and the time you have to enjoy it all.

As you take up the idea of talking about money in your family, consider a broader, more holistic definition of what wealth means. At my firm, we like to discuss four core facets of wealth: social capital, skills, time, and money.

Write down your assets in each of these categories to broaden your view of wealth.

1. Social Capital
   Example: A free babysitter on date night!
2. Skills
   Example: Carpentry or thrifting
3. Time
   Example: Lazy Sunday morning pancake breakfast
4. Money
   Example: A steady job or fully paid health care

Your baby may be tiny now, but they're learning all the time. You can help them develop an emotionally balanced and self-aware relationship with money, which will help them navigate their inevitable future questions of intrinsic worth in an extrinsic society.

SOME TIPS ON COLLEGE/TRADE SCHOOL/FUTURE FUNDING:

Avoid plastic stuff for your baby, and instead, fund their future! If it's a priority for your family, when your child is born, set up an account at your state's 529 college savings plan. They're generally well-managed and some states offer tax incentives.

They often have a gifting link you can share so family and friends can donate instead of giving toys or clothes they'll soon outgrow. Any amount is welcome when paired with the magic of tax-exempt, compound growth over the next 18 years!

Save for yourself first using the 4:1 rule. Match every dollar you contribute to your child's education fund with four dollars to your own retirement. Many parents want to put their kids first, but having a fully funded retirement account means you can take care of your own needs when you're older, allowing your child to be financially independent.

Talk about generosity with your kids. Discuss where you donate, any family members you financially support, or dollars you give to folks on the street. Generosity is like a muscle. When you exercise your generosity, you become a happier financial being. So help them learn it when they're young.

For more money tools and conversation guides, check out *Free Tools for the People* at modernistfinancial.com.

"By verbally processing financial decisions within their families, kids build architectures for financial decision-making that are explicit and practical."

Chapter 20

FREE RANGE(ISH) PARENTING.

How to give your little one space to explore.

Onikah Asamoa-Caesar is the founder and owner of Fulton Street Books & Coffee in Tulsa, Oklahoma. As a Daughter of the United States Middle Passage and an Enneagram 8, Onikah aspires to create and accelerate liberatory and communal change by approaching literacy as a tool for liberation. She is the proud mom of Hadassah and her two fur babies, Simba and Zazu.

She/Her	1 Kid	Woman	Black

TL;DR: It's instinctual for new parents to protect their children and rush to keep them safe from any possible harm. But sometimes, it's good to ask, how much danger are they *really* in? While it's important to keep our children safe, it's also important to encourage exploration and freedom for them to experience the world around them.

Because she was born during the COVID-19 pandemic, my daughter was already one and walking by the time she met her maternal grandmother. We were gathered in the living room and Hadassah was sitting on the floor in the midst of us all. It didn't take long for her to start exploring her surroundings, and by surroundings I mean her grandmother's trinkets and belongings.

She lifted her little hand to grab an item from the lower half of a china cabinet. As if on cue, a chorus of *aht-aht!* rang throughout the room. Everyone sprang toward her to ensure the trinket remained untouched.

At that moment, I wondered what messages we were sending her. The item she was reaching for was not something she could break, or harm herself or someone else with, and yet *aht-aht* reigned supreme. It was also in that moment that I doubled down on my desire to raise a free child.

Although Hadassah isn't old enough to walk to parks on her own or navigate city transportation, I hold a deep commitment to letting her explore freely and safely.

In our home, there is not a lot that is off-limits. Under a watchful eye, I let her open drawers and pull out clothes, I let her rummage through pots and pans, I let her sink her hands in the dirt in my house plants (often dispersing a handful across the floor), I let her climb up on the coffee table and sit there, I let her wiggle through the doggy door to get to the backyard (and I have even followed right behind her on an occasion or two).

I don't know how to measure the success of free-range parenting, but I do know that I want my daughter to *be*. Giving her range and autonomy is one way I validate her and show that I see her.

When I ask my friends to describe Hadassah, one thing seems to be true across the board. They believe her to be fearless. And, right now, that's enough for me.

"The item she was reaching for was not something she could break, or harm herself or someone else with, and yet *aht-aht* reigned supreme."

Chapter 21

RAISING A CURIOUS CHILD.

Using a scientific method for parenting to navigate uncertainty and make decisions.

Ara Katz is mom to a curious five-year-old named Pax and a brand-new baby named Zen. She credits her love of love, storytelling, nature, and discovery to her dad with whom she spent every weekend morning making movies, taking photos, building, and creating. Ara is the co-founder of Seed Health where she works to realize the potential of microbes for both human and planetary health. She lives in Venice, California, with her husband, Chris, where she continues the family legacy of cardboard box innovating and lots of time in nature. She is also the author of *A Kids Book About Your Microbiome*.

She/Her	2 Kids	Married	Female

TL;DR: Model curiosity, including in decision-making. A scientific method teaches us to lead with an open heart and mind. Experiment, learn, try again.

If we want to raise curious children, we must model curiosity as parents. This does not mean Googling "Why is the sky blue?" every time your inquisitive toddler asks a question.

What it *does* mean is finding a way to navigate the uncertainty of parenting, our own insecurities, and the millions of micro choices we make each day in our efforts to do our best as parents.

Of all the parenting books I read and advice I received, what I really wanted was a compass.

So, what if there were a scientific method for parenting?

Here's what I think the basic requirements would be:

- an open mind (and heart)
- a deep commitment to questioning (ask "why?" more than your toddler)
- rigorous data collection (remember, even your gut instinct is a data point!)
- a spirit of experimentation (you won't know until you try)
- a way of observing and learning (without sh*tting all over yourself)
- a way of being in the world that combats confirmation bias wherever possible

This means we don't just seek out "experts" (and those whom the algorithm serves to us) because they confirm our existing belief systems, but that we actively seek out different points of view to cultivate our *own* framework for the choices we make.

In Pax's first year, every decision felt like a big one. But when I had trouble breastfeeding after a few months, it was especially challenging given I work in an area of science that studies not only the importance of breast milk for a child's developing microbiome, but also the lifelong impact these early factors can have on a child's health.

So I used this approach to navigate my feelings of inadequacy, fear, and disappointment. My child had to get nourishment and I knew I wouldn't be the first mom in history to make this decision (despite how lonely parenting can feel at times).

First, as with any experiment, you need to do the underlying research to form your hypothesis. So I went back to the basics: What does my son need? What are the constituents of breast milk that can be replicated or approximated to meet those needs and what cannot be? What could I feel good about giving to Pax? What have other moms found to be effective? What has been researched? What do pediatricians with knowledge of these areas of science say?

I investigated every option, from the European "expensive stuff" to the moms smuggling raw Amish goat milk into discrete basement pickup spots in New York City, from the various peddlers of exotic animal milks (camel still tops the list) to human milk banks. Once I had all my data, I found the path that felt best informed and best for me and my son.

For me, parenting has been about incessant, persistent experimentation and iteration—learning by doing, feeling, and exploring. What better way to be of service than to parent with the same attributes we so badly want our children to have?

As for my personal experience (a concept that is too easily subverted as parents), this approach has made parenting enriching and alive for discovery. It has rekindled that "natural-born scientist" part of me that Carl Sagan says we are born with, but we lose as we grow up. It has cultivated a kind of fulfillment and depth that provides lasting, present connection in any given moment, anywhere. It has evolved my own way of being in the world. Most importantly, it has empowered me to make choices that can feel informed and optimistic (even when I'm wrong).

It's applicable for the little moments—like looking at a bug or pondering why the sky is blue—and for the big topics like sugar, vaccines, and sleep.

And yes, in the middle of a seven-night, no-sleep streak of dealing with tantrums and the feeling of "I don't think I can do this one more day," this may sound esoteric. But it has, even in the hardest moments, empowered me to know that this cyclical journey of question > research > hypothesize > experiment > observe > learn is always available to me.

And that if this methodology led to the discovery of gravity, codified Newtonian physics, and informed some of our greatest truths, perhaps we can employ it to not only discover our best inner parent, but much about ourselves in the process.

"For me, parenting has been about incessant, persistent experimentation and iteration— learning by doing, feeling, and exploring."

Chapter 22

CHOICES AROUND EQUITY.

How to prioritize diversity in your baby's life.

Stephen Green is a Black-Latino person living in the Pacific Northwest. He and his wife are focused on preparing their three children to live out their dreams in a world that is often intent on crushing them. They believe it's hard to be what you don't see, so they know representation is key in helping their kids reach their goals.

He/Him	3 Kids	Married	Black & Latino

TL;DR: Make it a priority to show your child a diverse world. Your actions now, even when they are infants, will leave an imprint on your child's future.

You'll quickly start to notice your kids are always listening and learning, even when they're tiny. They take their cues from you, and the life you live will lay a path for your kid to follow.

Upon becoming a parent, I wanted to be intentional about my choices around equity and racism. My wife and I started considering our decisions long before we held our first kid in our arms. We wondered how we could discuss race and the impacts of racism honestly. How could we empower them to advocate for those who are historically and socially disadvantaged?

To start, we chose to live in a diverse neighborhood so our family could be around as many diverse perspectives and cultures as possible. That isn't the only option. If you live in a homogeneous neighborhood, be intentional about diversity. Take your baby to diverse places, and let them see a variety of skin colors and hear languages and words that are different from your own.

When they're big enough, encourage them to taste foods from different cultures and learn about where their food comes from. Talk about how it might be different from the food you prepare at home. This helps them understand that *different* doesn't mean *bad* or *less than*. You'll be surprised how curious babies can be and how much they enjoy seeing differences in others. When you encourage this exploration, you broaden their worldview.

Kids will be aware of what you teach them to be cognizant of. Be mindful of what your little one sees and hears. How do you talk to your neighbor? What are you watching on TV? Who are your friends? Choose intentionally.

George Floyd's murder and the racially charged events of 2020 woke my wife and I up to the fact that being an anti-racist is more than not using racial slurs. Go beyond being an ally for social justice and do the work of participating in social justice *change.*

If you are a person of color and there aren't people in your life who look like you, find them. If your doctors or bankers or lawyers don't look like you, think about what it would mean for your kid and their understanding of themselves if some of them did.

If you are white, think about whether there are professionals in your life who are people of color. If there aren't, do something about it. Be intentional and demonstrate that not everyone in a professional setting looks like you, and that's a good thing.

Valuing diversity takes constant stewardship, and things do change over time. Plant the seed early and help grow the young human being you want out in the world.

"You'll be surprised how curious babies can be and how much they enjoy seeing differences in others."

SECTION TWO
THE BABY.

By now, it's clear your baby didn't come with an instruction manual. Your biggest teachers will likely be your little one and your own instincts, but you'll be asking many questions to doctors and midwives and the internet as well. As a parent, making informed decisions matters. How do you swaddle a baby? Are all germs bad? No matter how serious or trivial your concerns, they will feel like mountains at first. So, put on your climbing shoes.

This section of the book walks you through the care of your baby. This might be the part you flip through while your little one is having trouble napping or you are getting ready for their first bath. In those moments, when you're not sure whose advice to take, remember you're not the first person to experience it (whatever it is), you will get through it, and make sure to enjoy the ride.

Chapter 23

QUESTIONS FOR THE DOCTOR.

Answers to your questions about your baby's fragility, burping, crying, pacifiers, and formula, from a doctor *and* parent.

Dr. Tracey Agnese is a board-certified pediatrician and has been a practicing physician on the Upper West Side in Manhattan for over ten years. She received her undergraduate degree from the University of Delaware, her medical school degree from SUNY Downstate, and completed her pediatrics residency at NYU. You may find her online at @babydocmama and traceymd.com.

She/Her	2 Kids	Married

TL;DR: From fears about hurting your baby, to burping techniques, to general encouragement from a professional AND parent, find comfort and advice in the words of this experienced doctor.

A doctor's disclaimer: Although Tracey Agnese, MD, is a licensed physician, this information is for general informational purposes only and is not medical advice. Never disregard professional medical advice and/or delay in seeking medical attention because of something you may have read here. Always seek advice from a qualified medical professional, especially if your baby is ever refusing to feed, very uncomfortable with feeding, has projectile vomiting, is inconsolable, has a fever (100.4 or above rectally), or has blood in their stool. If you have any other concerns, please call your child's doctor immediately.

Even as a pediatrician, I was shocked at how hard it was to take care of a newborn baby. I finished medical school and was already practicing general pediatrics in New York City for several years before I had my first child. Yet, I still felt unprepared when taking her home from the hospital. I left thinking, "Really, they're just gonna let me leave with her?" Now, with real-world experience under my belt in addition to my medical training, I love helping new parents simplify baby care and feel confident in their abilities.

I know that each decision you have to make as new parents seems like a really big one. But for the most part, there are no right or wrong answers; there's just what's best for your family right now. This may change with time, and that's okay. Your baby is adjusting to this world, and you're learning how to be a parent. Enjoy the process of learning together!

Let's take a look at some of the most common questions I get from new parents.

My baby is so small, and seems so fragile—will I hurt them accidentally?

Your baby is not as fragile as you think! Really, it's true. New parents are always concerned about this. They worry about burping their baby incorrectly, hurting the soft spot on their head, or pulling their baby's arm out of its socket. When new parents see me burp a baby their jaws often drop at how firmly I do it. And softly kissing and gently touching the soft spot on their head is totally fine too!

I promise, you are not going to hurt your baby with routine baby care, and you will get more comfortable handling your little one over time. That's the thing I love so much about babies—they're resilient little creatures. Your baby isn't made of glass.

What's the best way to burp my baby? How often? What if the baby doesn't burp?

The traditional advice is to burp your baby during and after each feeding. Babies swallow air during feeding and that air can make them spit up, be gassy, and feel uncomfortable. So you need to burp them to help them get rid of that air.

You can start by burping every time you switch breasts if nursing, or halfway through the feeding if you're using a bottle (which is usually after a few ounces). Then, burp the baby again when they're all finished feeding. If you try burping for a few minutes and there's no burp, don't worry about it! The gas will come out the other end eventually.

Burping a baby is simple and there are many ways to do it. Please don't worry about doing it wrong—you really can't. You'll eventually figure out what your baby likes.

Here are a few common burping positions you can start with. They all involve keeping the baby upright while you rub or pat their back.

- The classic over-your-shoulder. Position your baby tummy toward you, with head and neck supported.
- Have your baby sitting on your lap while your hand is under their chin.
- Put your baby face down in your lap and support the baby's head so it's a little higher than their chest.

In any of these positions, you can pat or rub the baby's back. Your inclination as a new parent is to be gentle, so I find that saying this as a reminder just scares parents unnecessarily! In actuality, I often find myself telling parents it's okay to rub or pat harder.

You can try any of these techniques to rub or pat:

- Across the shoulder blades or toward the left side of the baby's back.
- In circles or upward.
- Using the palm or heel of your hand.

- Massaging the baby.
- Leaning the baby slightly more forward while putting some pressure on the belly with your hand.
- Laying your baby on their back and gently cycling their legs toward their chest like they are pedaling a bicycle.

There are so many ways you can try to burp your baby. And if you do, always have a burp cloth handy because spit up happens.

But here's a little secret: there's no good evidence you have to do any of this! I've found that for some babies, burping doesn't really help and can cause *more* spit up. Honestly, doesn't that kind of make sense? If someone hit you on the back after you ate, I don't think you would enjoy it. And you might spit up a little too.

Bottom line: If you want to burp your baby, go for it! If your baby is fussy and gassy and crying, definitely give it a try. If still fussy or gassy, you can try burping more or less. But if you find that it doesn't make a difference or that your baby is better off without it, don't worry. And if no burp comes out no matter how much you try, don't worry about that either.

Why won't my baby stop crying?

Part of the reason we burp babies is because we often don't know exactly why babies are crying. So we do everything we can as new parents to try to stop that crying. And since eating, pooping, and sleeping are the only activities babies really do in the beginning, we assume their crying has to do with one of those things. And a lot of times, it does!

Take gas, for example. Babies are gassy for many reasons. Their digestive systems are immature, and since their tummies are so small and they eat frequently, their digestive systems are working day and night. Gas is a natural byproduct of a busy digestive system and usually improves as babies get older and are able to take in more at each feeding, allowing their digestive systems to rest in between feeds.

Babies also make lots of funny, weird faces. This makes them look like they're in pain, especially when they're pooping or burping. But that doesn't mean either is hurting them. When you poop, your body has to contract certain muscles while relaxing others—try doing that while lying on your back! If the poop is soft when it comes out, your baby is not having a hard time pooping. They're just learning.

Remember that all of these bodily sensations are new to your baby and they're just getting used to them. Passing gas can be startling when you're first learning what that feels like.

And often, babies aren't crying because of any of those things. Life outside the womb is a big adjustment for your little baby. The first three months of a baby's life can be thought of as the fourth trimester. During this time, they're often most comforted by mimicking life inside the womb. That's why things like swaddling, rocking, white noise, sucking on a pacifier or thumb, and holding them positioned on their side or tummy can ease fussiness.

Even with your best efforts, most babies cry more during the first three months of life than at any other time. You can do everything right and your baby will still cry! But as parents, we are always looking to find the problem so we can fix it and help them stop crying.

If you go through the checklist and your baby still cries, you should check with your baby's doctor. If the baby checks out okay and is growing well, know this will get better with time.

Are pacifiers okay to use?

I say yes, pacifiers are fine! Sucking is a calming reflex babies develop in the womb, so it's a great way to calm them when they're fussy. Still, there are a lot of questions and concerns from new parents about when and how to use (or stop using) a pacifier.

Parents worry about pacifiers interfering with nursing, but there's really no good evidence that suggests this. If you're having trouble getting your baby to latch on and you choose to hold off on the pacifier for now, that's totally fine too!

Parents worry their baby will get used to the pacifier, cry when it falls out at night, and they'll have to keep going in to replace it. This is definitely possible! But it's usually only a short window of time until babies are able to put the paci back in themselves.

Parents worry about having to ultimately stop their baby from relying on a pacifier. But let me tell you, babies who enjoy non-nutritive sucking for self-soothing will often find a thumb or a finger if the pacifier isn't there. And that's much harder to get rid of than a pacifier!

Parents worry because they can't get their baby to use a pacifier. Try different brands and styles to find one which suits your child best. Paci or no paci...if your baby just refuses, that's okay too!

Is it okay to give my baby formula?

The short answer is yes, absolutely! We are fortunate to have more than one safe way to feed our babies and meet all their nutritional requirements.

The long answer is, breast milk is the optimal source of nutrition for newborn babies. It has the perfect ingredients for your baby, offers protection from certain infections, and has many other intangible added benefits. If you can, take a minute to read up about the science of breast milk because it's amazing what the human body can do!

That being said, I'm here to tell you it's okay if you can't or choose not to give your baby breast milk for any reason, or you want or need to give them both breast milk and formula.

Feeding your baby is a choice which should consider more than just nutrition. Each baby has their own unique needs, and you will find your own unique way of providing for them.

Breastfeeding is not easy and it doesn't come naturally to many people. It takes a lot of support, technique, encouragement, coordination, and dedication. If breastfeeding is something your family has chosen to do, I always recommend getting all the help you can early on. That could include lactation consultants, nurses, physicians, family members, and friends. The first two weeks are the hardest, so try to push through that period before deciding it's not for you, because most times, it does get much easier for both you and your baby.

If you can give some breast milk but have to supplement with formula, please feel proud of every drop you are able to provide.

If you choose to pump and give that to your baby, great work.

But if breastfeeding doesn't work out, feel proud of your efforts and decision.

There are many valid reasons people do not give their baby breast milk.

Sometimes:
- It's just not possible for that family from the start.
- The parent's physical health prohibits it.
- The parent's mental health needs to take priority.
- The baby doesn't get the hang of it.
- The baby's physical health prohibits it.
- Parents simply choose not to.

Whatever the reason, you don't owe an explanation to anyone. Only you know what's best for your family right now.

However you choose to feed your baby, enjoy the process. While holding your newborn in your arms and seeing those precious little eyes stare back at you, recognize that any way you nourish your baby is beautiful.

✓	Questions For The Doctor

Chapter 24

DIAPERING.

Many options for diapers, one bottom of truth.

Altimese Nichole is the founder of The Ezer Agency, a Minority Business Enterprise certified public relations and marketing firm. She is also a best-selling author, speaker, and single mommy to a witty, brave mini-human whom she calls Izzy Busy. Of all her titles and accolades, the one she holds with the most regard is "mommy."

She/Her	1 Kid	Divorced	African American

TL;DR: Trial and error can be a great way to find the best diaper for your baby, and ultimately, their reaction (and their bottom) matters most.

Purchasing diapers for your baby seems like a simple, even unimportant part of the parental decision-making process. Of course, we want our babies to be happy, kind contributors to the world, but our main job is to keep them alive and well.

Diapers are the covering to your baby's most intimate, sensitive areas. Yes, they catch pee and poop. They also provide a sense of protection for your child. While the safest place for new babies will be skin-to-skin contact, right next to your heart, the products you choose matter and help ensure your baby feels a sense of safety and protection. In short, diapers can be a big deal.

When purchasing diapers, pay attention to your baby's response. Do they wiggle in discomfort? Do they seem irritated after a diaper change? When my daughter was born, we continued using the hospital diapers for some time. But after watching plenty of commercials and advertisements about diapers, I thought, "Could there be a better diaper than this one?"

Then one brave grocery shopping day, I strolled past the brand I always used and ventured toward the others. There were so many to choose from, and the prices varied from affordable to excessive. As a new mom, this felt a bit overwhelming, but I made my initial decision based on what I had heard and seen—the rest of my assessment was based on observation of my daughter's reaction.

Like so many firsts in parenthood, buying diapers is a try-and-see process. Here are a few things I learned when making that transition to new diapers for the first time.

Size.
First, the new diapers appeared to take up less space and fit a little smaller, but they were supposedly the same size. Odd.

Texture.
The new diapers were also more textured to the touch. As I rubbed my hand over the inside of the diaper, I could feel the woven fibers more. It felt like the diaper was just more natural. This could be a good thing, right?

Closures.
The tabs reminded me of a kind of velcro that can really only be used once. If you adjust it twice, or three times for the brave ones, the sticky part will not hold as tightly.

My kid's butt.
My final decision was based on my daughter's butt. I knew her butt. I knew her peeing and pooping schedule, I knew how many wipes I would need, and I knew her response after a diaper change.

What I learned was these diapers were smaller, the fibers were looser, and she went through more of them than the original ones. And, there seemed to be less overall coverage when I changed her. So, I went back to the original diapers.

The marketing worked at first, but our personal experience held the most importance.

The bottom line is *learn thy baby*. Study them like a new skill you want to hone. And remember, what works for some babies may not work for yours. And that's how it should be!

Different bottoms require different care.

EXTRA TIP: You will have random, lingering diapers because your baby decides to grow mid-box. Donate those to a local women's shelter or offer them to another parent with a baby who can fit in them.

"...I made my initial decision based on what I had heard and seen— the rest of my assessment was based on observation of my daughter's reaction."

Chapter 25

CAR SEATS.

Don't let the car seat intimidate you.

Ryan Tillman is a dad of three—Grayson (7), Gavin (5), and Ryland (2). He is married to Kimberly and they reside in Eastvale, which is located in Southern California. Ryan is a police officer and owner of Breaking Barriers United, an organization created to bridge the gap between law enforcement and the community.

3 Kids	Black

TL;DR: How do you know if your car seat is set up correctly? Read the manual, follow the instructions, look up that tutorial, and ask someone to check your work.

As a new parent, situations can become overwhelming very quickly, especially as it pertains to child safety. The balancing act of being the "overprotective" parent and the parent who allows their child to do something dangerous can sometimes feel like a day-to-day struggle.

If you deliver your baby at a hospital or birthing center, you are immediately faced with your first test of being a responsible parent—safely transporting your precious cargo back to your home. The moment of truth will arrive and you'll ask yourself, Do I feel safe about having my baby in this car seat?

But don't worry, stick with me and I will help you successfully conquer this first challenge as a new parent. Mastering the car seat can remind you that although you may not have it all figured out as a parent (who does?), with some patience and practice, you can overcome any obstacle.

Here is a simple checklist to make sure your child is buckled in safely!

Step 1: Purchase the correct car seat.
Car seats are distinguished by age and weight requirements. At the infant stage, the car seat needs to be installed facing the rear of the car. As your child grows, the car seat should be installed to face the front of the car. Check the car seat requirements and ask your pediatrician for guidance based on your baby's age and weight development.

It's also worth mentioning that you should check your local and state vehicle code regulations to assure your car seat meets the proper requirements for child restraint systems. Most of this information can be found online.

Step 2: Practice before baby's arrival.
There are so many things to plan for as a new parent, and planning for the first ride home is so important. Upon buying the new car seat, read the instructions for the seat installation as well as the sections about car seats in your vehicle manual.

With the advancement of technology, there are tutorials for everything. It may be worth looking up the make and model of your car seat to see if there is a tutorial available online to assist you with installing it.

Step 3: Always double-check your work.
Ask someone you know and trust like your partner, parents, or friends with kids to come and give the car seat a tug once you've completed the installation. What feels secure for you may not feel secure for your trusted team.

Check your local police or fire department. Many locations host car seat safety days and will check your installation to be sure it's safe.

Step 4: Keep the car keys with you.

Never place your keys or your bag with your keys in it in the car before you get in. Keep them with you until you are ready to start the car and get going.

Step 5: Enjoy the moment.

One minute you will be purchasing a newborn car seat, the next minute it will be a toddler seat, and, before you know it, your child will ride safely buckled in the passenger seat, right next to you! As always, check your state and local guidelines and with your pediatrician regarding when it is safe for your child to make these moves.

There's no doubt that being a new parent is stressful, but the faster you realize that being a perfect parent is not the destination but rather a journey, the sooner you can enjoy it.

Safe travels, my friends.

"The moment of truth will arrive and you'll ask yourself, Do I feel safe about having my baby in this car seat?"

Chapter 26

SCREENS.

Finding a healthy balance with screen time.

Anya Kamenetz lives in Brooklyn with two daughters, a cat, and her husband. She covers education for National Public Radio (NPR), and her books include *The Art Of Screen Time* and *The Stolen Year*, about children and COVID. She is an aerial acrobat and is happiest in a hoop upside down.

She/Her	2 Kids	Married	Jewish

TL;DR: How do you let technology into your baby's world while ensuring it won't take over? Believe it or not, there is bad screen time *and* good screen time.

From the day they are born, your baby seeks eye contact with you.[1] Eye contact is a powerful form of bonding, and it's part of the process of falling in love. For babies, tracking the gaze of others is one important way they learn about the world and the people in it.

However, grownups have been carrying a black mirror in their pockets everywhere for the better part of the past two decades. When our gaze[2] disappears into our devices too often, we introduce into the parent-baby dynamic what scientists call *technoference*.[3] This tech interference can later lead to behavioral problems in kids. Why? When the distractions and stress of screens are around, you don't talk or sing to your baby as much. You don't respond as quickly or as skillfully when they're upset. These little moments add up.

Screens.

On the other hand, tech is a part of our lives, and we need to help our children discover its possibilities—not just its dangers. How? Don't despair; parents are not failing when they let their baby engage with a device. Research shows even infants can benefit from up to twenty minutes a day of interaction with an electronic device. Here are some things that can create mindful harmony where screens and tiny humans must coexist.

- When you're with your baby, try not to play the TV in the background.[4] Music or other audio is a better choice. Background noise from TVs can diminish the quality and quantity of your interactions with baby.
- Designate specific times to look at your phone, like during nap time or when your baby is fully engaged in play by themselves.
- Set notifications and alerts for critical messages only.
- When you pick up your phone, include your baby by letting them know why. For example, say, "Let's check the weather!" or, "I want to find a good smoothie recipe."
- When you are taking a photo, consider using the selfie camera so your baby can interact and enjoy the view.
- Opt for video chat with a beloved person who is far away, allowing them to connect eye to eye with baby.

"When our gaze disappears into our devices too often, we introduce into the parent-baby dynamic what scientists call *technoference*."

[1]National Academy of Sciences, *Eye contact detection in humans from birth*. 0PNAS, 2002) https://www.pnas.org/content/99/14/9602.short
[2]The National Center for Biotechnology Information, *Social and emotional contexts predict the development of gaze following in early infancy* (NCBI, 2020) https://www.ncbi.nlm.nih.gov/pmc/articles/PMC7540771
[3]Society for Research in Child Development, *Technoference: Parent Distraction With Technology and Associations With Child Behavior Problems* (SRCD, 2017)
[4]Society for Research in Child Development, *The Impact of Background Television on Parent-Child Interaction* (SRCD, 2009) https://srcd.onlinelibrary.wiley.com/doi/abs/10.1111/j.1467-8624.2009.01337.x

Chapter 27

GO OUTSIDE.

Little one, meet the great outdoors.

Paul J. Pastor is a book guy (author, editor, reader) and an outdoor guy (hiker, gardener, forager) living in one of Oregon's most beautiful wild places: the Columbia River Gorge. He's husband to Emily, and dad to Elaia (11), Emmaus (9), and Marko (7).

He/Him	3 Kids	Married

TL;DR: Protect your baby from real harm, but allowing them to explore and get a little dirty outside teaches them about risk assessment, the natural world, and that they are a part of something bigger than themselves.

I hate to break it to you, but right now, your baby is probably not living in their natural habitat.

Our contemporary world has wonderful things to offer. Toilet paper, anyone? Donuts? But it tends to come at a high cost. We've gotten used to living in human-defined environments—climate-controlled, never uncomfortable, and sanitary to the point of being sterile. The splinters sanded off, rough edges covered, the dirt quickly wiped out of our kids' drooly little mouths when they take a bite of a freshly baked mud pie. The truth is, we humans lose something vital when we lose connection with the wilder parts of ourselves—and that's also true of our kids.

Fortunately, there's a solution. *Go outside.*

Go Outside.

There's no right way or time to do it. You just do it. It can be as small as a planter on a patio or as large as the Pacific Ocean. Let them lay, flop, scoot, crawl, sploosh, and toddle across the grass, muck, rock, snow, and sand. See time outside as learning, and every bit as important as any other learning they are doing.

Your kid will be looking to you for cues any time you're outside. Model for them that people are made to be outside. That it's okay to be too cold, or too hot, for a little while. That they're tougher than they might think. That dirt will wash out, and scrapes will scab up. That sometimes there are amazing chores to be done. That sometimes there is an amazing walk to be had. That sometimes all that's needed is to be. That this is *life*!

Will there be some risk? Yes. Your baby will get cut, stung, irritated, scratched, bruised, bopped, thumped, and generally roughed up. Through that, they will be learning how to manage risk, how the real physics of rocks and logs and sand and leaves and feathers work, and how good this all is.

As they grow, the safest kids are generally the ones who were allowed to get hurt on their own a bit as babies! Over-parenting outside—except to prevent real injury—can backfire long-term, ultimately creating kids who don't really understand risk.

And through it all, your baby will learn how much they belong here. They will see the world directly, not through a screen. They will not just be a visitor to this wonderful, wild, scary, amazing world of nature. They will be home, in their natural habitat. And you'll be right there with them.

"Let them lay, flop, scoot, crawl, sploosh, and toddle across the grass, muck, rock, snow, and sand."

Chapter 28

SWADDLING.

The how-to of swaddling baby and why it's so important.

Rick DeLucco is a graphic designer, illustrator, and most importantly, a father of two sons, George and Enzo. After being around the block a couple times, he's learned some tips and tricks for the early parenting process.

He/Him	2 Kids	Married	Heterosexual

TL;DR: Swaddling isn't for every baby but can calm those who need that sense of closeness and security they felt in the womb.

For a new parent, swaddling your child for the first time can feel awkward. Not only are you desperately trying to get the hang of it and not break your baby, but it feels like you're wrapping them up like a little mummy.

Is this comfortable? Is it too tight? Does my baby even like this?

Rest assured, swaddling might be exactly what your baby needs to, well, rest. Believe it or not, the snug hold feels comforting, providing them with a close and cuddly feeling which helps them to sleep. And while they're peacefully snoozing in their crib you can, I don't know, go to the bathroom, eat, maybe doze off yourself—imagine that!

Keep in mind that some babies might not want to be swaddled, and that's okay too.

Swaddling can be complicated. Let's break it down into steps so you *and* baby can get some much-needed rest.

Secrets of the Perfect Swaddle:

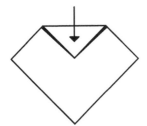

1. Spread a light blanket out and fold the top corner over.

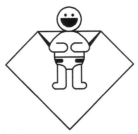

2. Lay baby face-up, their neck aligned with the folded corner.

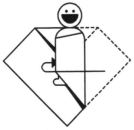

3. Wrap the right corner over and tuck it under their body.

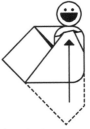

4. Bring the bottom corner up and tuck it into the top of the blanket near baby's head.

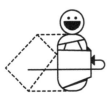

5. Wrap the left corner over baby so that it lays flat under their body.

Voila! Don't worry if you don't get it on your first try—practice makes perfect. And believe me, when you're under pressure and desperation kicks in, you'll become a pro!

FUN FACT: Our second baby, Enzo, was a bit of an escape artist when it came to swaddling. We ended up purchasing and trying out every swaddler on the market—and there were a lot. It's incredible how many versions of this you can find out there. We eventually found one that was right for us, and it ended up keeping our little Houdini snug!

Chapter 29

COMMUNICATION BEFORE LANGUAGE.

Learning to communicate with all the senses.

Cherie Ulmer is the mother of three grown boys. She is a CODA—Child of Deaf Adults—and served as a child development specialist for deaf and hard of hearing students at the Oregon School for the Deaf for almost thirty years.

She/Her	3 Kids	Single

TL;DR: Exposing your baby to communication by utilizing all of the senses enriches and deepens their ability to communicate.

A newborn fresh from the womb faces a rush of new stimulation: sights, sounds, smells, eventually tastes, and always, always touch. Each sensation brings experience. Experience is education. Education fosters language.

As you hold your infant securely wrapped in soft blankets, they sense warmth and safety. As you sing or coo, your baby will sense what love sounds like. With your smile or tilt of your head, the child will visualize and eventually mimic your movements. Playing peekaboo will produce laughter from your child. All of this is direct, unfiltered communication.

Babies soon recognize that you are called mama or papa; before long, they will test out those syllables and sounds on their lips.

Close to their first birthday, they will deliver their first words. If you intentionally and consistently use gestures or signs paired with spoken words at this early age, children will naturally imitate the same gesture or sign when they speak those words.

An open hand with the thumb touching the chin or forehead is the American Sign Language (ASL) sign for mom or dad. I learned ASL from my Deaf parents and used it later with my own three boys. My sons and I also played word games, matching the word *milk* with the corresponding sign—a pantomime of sorts—akin to milking a cow. This was a source of much laughter and playful learning.

Some parents of Deaf children are hesitant to expose their kids to sign language as they fear the child will lose the desire or ability to use spoken language. Rest assured: the opposite will occur! Children who are exposed to multiple languages, aural or visual, in the window of maximum language acquisition will only enrich their language and communication abilities.

That window of opportunity for the most language development is within the first three years of a child's life. So, it is never too early to expose children to communication using all the senses. For example, using an early visual model like cards with black and white images, while simultaneously talking about what's on the card, can stimulate cognitive functioning more holistically. I often refer to my own bilingual upbringing as "thinking in 3D."

So, sign! Sing! Dance! Read poetry out loud! Milk a cow! Celebrate any and all communication you have with your child. You are building a foundation for your baby that makes learning and communicating fun.

"Children who are exposed to several languages, aural or visual, in the window of maximum language acquisition will only enrich their language and communication abilities."

Chapter 30

DENTAL CARE.

Even before they have teeth, dental care matters.

Vanessa Coupet, DMD, is a pediatric dentist born in Brooklyn, New York. She received her bachelor of arts degree from Cornell University and a dental degree from Tufts University School of Dental Medicine. She completed her general and pediatric dental residencies at Bronx Lebanon Hospital. Vanessa is currently a pediatric dentist and an assistant professor at Weill Cornell Medical College/New York Presbyterian Hospital and serves as the dental consultant at St. Mary's Hospital for Children in Bayside, New York.

She/Her	Black

TL;DR: Teeth or no teeth, dental care starts as soon as milk or formula consumption begins (in other words, from day one). Not only does this help baby build healthy oral hygiene but it creates a positive relationship with the often-dreaded dentist's office.

It's important to care for your baby's mouth starting from birth, before teeth begin erupting through their gums. Practicing healthy habits from the beginning can prevent cavities and help build lifelong oral habits that will also support their overall health.

Twenty baby teeth are already present in the jaw at birth and, on average, usually begin to emerge starting around six months of age. Most children have all twenty baby teeth by the time they are three years old.

However, even before your baby has teeth, it is recommended to keep their gums clean. You can wipe their gums at least twice a day—in the morning after the first feeding, and right before bed. One way to do this is to wrap a clean, moistened soft washcloth around one of your fingers and gently massage the gum tissues.

Between the ages of six and twelve months, when your baby's first tooth erupts, the gums may be swollen and saliva flow may increase. This may cause your baby some discomfort. To ease these symptoms, give them a clean teething ring, especially those that can be refrigerated or frozen. Cold temperatures are soothing and will help alleviate the discomfort.

It is also recommended that your baby should have their first dental visit within six months after the eruption of the first primary tooth or no later than twelve months of age.

When brushing their teeth, use a small, soft toothbrush with a tiny amount of fluoride toothpaste. The fluoride in toothpaste helps strengthen the tooth enamel. When children are young and don't know how to spit yet, you should wipe out the excess toothpaste with a piece of wet gauze or washcloth. Toothpaste should never be swallowed.

Much like your own daily dental care, brushing your baby's teeth should be the last step every night before bed.

"Even before your child has teeth, it is recommended to keep their gums clean."

We all believe in you!

Chapter 31

BOTTLE FEEDING.

When breastfeeding isn't the best choice for your family.

D. L. Mayfield is a writer and neighbor who lives with her two kids, two cats, and therapist husband on the edge of Portland, Oregon.

She/Her	2 Kids	Married	Autistic

TL;DR: New parents can often feel that there is a "right" way to do things, and when we aren't able to achieve those goals for whatever reason, we feel like failures. Developing a plan B and using it when needed makes that plan the best one.

Here's how I learned that bottle feeding is a miracle and became comfortable treating it as such.

When I was pregnant, I scoured books and blogs to make sure I could do everything "right." For me, that meant aiming for a natural childbirth, breastfeeding for as long as possible, and generally trying to stay away from anything involving too much plastic.

But when I was thirty-three weeks pregnant, I became incredibly ill and needed to deliver my baby by emergency C-section. My daughter, thankfully, was fine—tiny, but healthy. This experience was my first introduction to the unpredictability of parenthood.

I tried to pump breast milk for the first three weeks of her life in between resting and getting a chance to hold her. Finally, I had to admit to myself that it just wasn't working.

I had nothing to give.

I sobbed and sobbed, releasing all my pent-up emotions from the entire experience. My body was a failure. I was a failure. My tiny little baby needed everything possible to thrive, and I couldn't provide it.

A kind nurse pulled me aside and told me my body had been through too much and to give it grace. She pointed to my husband snuggling our daughter in a hospital chair. He was feeding her out of the tiniest bottle I had ever seen. "All the nurses love watching him," she told me. And I saw him through her eyes—I watched my husband take care of my daughter in a way that was tangible and physical.

My grief at pivoting to bottle feeding didn't go away overnight. But eventually, I was able to see that the plan B for feeding our child had some positives I had never considered. For example, my husband, mom, dad, and sisters all got to be a part of feeding and caring for my daughter—it was a communal endeavor. Becoming a part of the bottle-feeding community also brought me closer to other people in my city and around the globe who have needed or chose to rely on the miracle that is formula.

Bottle feeding might not have felt like the best option initially, but it was just what our family needed. And that made it perfect for us.

"My body was a failure. I was a failure. My tiny little baby needed everything possible to thrive, and I couldn't do it."

Chapter 32

NURTURING.

On holding your baby close.

Ethan Thrower is a Black father of two children, a husband, and an alternative school social worker. He is a formerly incarcerated person and author of *A Kids Book About Incarceration*. He works and lives in Portland, Oregon.

He/Him	2 Kids	Married	Black

TL;DR: Nurturing love takes focus and connection. Establishing caring practices that make sense for you and your child builds trust and a sense of safety and belonging that will help your baby emotionally thrive.

I remember my very first night holding my brand-new baby. I held my daughter on my chest and felt a lifetime of "be tough" conditioning melt away.

Before you had your baby, do you remember the type of parent you hoped to be? I do! At the top of my list was to be a nurturing father. I spent far too many years of my life in an environment absent of emotional connection. My life experiences in young adulthood created a hardened version of me I didn't want to shape my parenting.

You might be thinking, Isn't nurturing automatic when you're a parent? Well, I have found that nurturing takes intentionality and vulnerability. Allow yourself to slow down, tune out the frenzy you might be experiencing, and just connect with your new baby. What messages do you want to send them? How will you communicate "I love you" and "You're safe with me" and

"I'm here for you"? This communication happens even before they understand the words.

For me, nurturing was holding my babies close, it was using a calming voice, it was singing, it was wearing the baby carrier, it was eye contact, it was smiling, it was telling them words of love.

You may feel like nurturing is a big concept, and it is! It's okay to keep it simple. Just have fun establishing your unique bond. Know that it will be perfect in the moment and then evolve over time. When you nurture your new baby, you make a difference.

Studies show that nurturing babies helps them feel calmer, sleep better, and cry less. Nurturing also plays a role in healthy brain development and social-emotional skills.[1]

My daughters are now five and nine years old. They share their feelings with me, they ask for help and comforting hugs, they enjoy when I sing their special songs to them.

There are stages of raising a child that come and go quickly. Make nurturing your child permanent and ever-present from the beginning. Hold your baby close and introduce them to a relationship rooted in unconditional love, safety, and connection. Be authentic and let your actions come from your heart. Nurture them to the moon and back. I do.

"You might be thinking, Isn't nurturing automatic as a parent?"

[1]Ruth Slocum, Jens Jespersen, and Amanda Sheffield Morris, "Nurturing Your Baby's Social and Emotional Growth - Oklahoma State University," Nurturing Your Baby's Social and Emotional Growth | Oklahoma State University (Oklahoma State University, August 1, 2020), https://extension.okstate.edu/fact-sheets/nurturing-your-babys-social-and-emotional-growth.html.

Chapter 33

PLAY AND DEVELOPMENT.

Use play as a tool to learn with your baby and practice joy.

Jennifer (Jen) White-Johnson is an Afro-Latina, disabled artist and designer living in Baltimore, Maryland. She lives with her eight-year-old Autistic son, Knox, and her husband, Kevin. Jen loves taking photos, making zines, practicing her ukulele, and using design to activate social change within the disability community.

She/Her	1 Kid	Married	Afro-Latina

TL;DR: Play looks different for every family and it's about much more than just fun. Playtime is also a time to nurture acceptance, heal, and practice radical joy.

I knew my parenting journey would be unique when my son was born at thirty-one weeks, weighing 2 pounds, 15 ounces. My pregnancy was smooth until then and I was unprepared for a preterm birth experience.

I'll never forget the day I took Knox home after spending forty-five days in the NICU. He continued to thrive and grow every day, and I quickly learned that once I stopped putting pressure on myself, the best medicine I could give my baby was love, care, and the freedom of fun.

Although we received amazing support from our NICU nurses, once we left, we knew it was time to put in the work to help him thrive. Looking back, I don't know how I managed it all along with my anxiety and ADHD behaviors. As preemie parents, it was easy to get caught up in making comparisons of our son's development to other full-term kids. We grew nervous each time he didn't meet his developmental milestones. I had to remember that being a preemie meant he was on his own timeline.

Through that experience, I learned a lot about how to play with my son during the first year of his life. Play and joy are an opportunity to embrace your child's differences and exist with them in their own unique space of freedom.

Here's a blueprint:
- Make playtime immersive and interactive.
- Don't stifle or hide your own inner child.
- Create your own play rituals.
- Don't be afraid to get messy.
- Sing a lot—it helps with language development.
- Encourage spontaneity and authenticity.
- Bring art and creativity into your play practice.
- Playtime may bring up old emotions for you, so hold space for your own vulnerabilities and trauma.
- Create room for your baby's authenticity—play can be a time for teaching acceptance.
- Remember that joy is an act of resistance; use it to honor your baby's disabilities or differences.

For me and my son, love, care, and lots of play was the best way to help him thrive and grow into the beautiful child he is today. Don't put pressure on yourself to know everything there is to know about being a parent as soon as your baby arrives. Instead, use play as a way to learn who your baby is, what their needs are, and how to help them learn.

EXTRA TIP: Babies and toddlers, including those who will later be diagnosed as a person with Autism, comfort themselves through repetitive stimulating behaviors called stimming. Stimming can be a form of purposeful play which creates safe space for dancing, spinning, bouncing, clapping, singing, and finding joy and comfort in repetitive behaviors and sounds.

Chapter 34

LANGUAGE ACQUISITION.

How to encourage a verbal child during everyday activities.

Shari Harpaz is a proud single mother of a five-year old. She's a speech-language pathologist based in New York City who works with very young children. Raised by parents who immigrated to the US, she was taught that with love surrounding you, anything is possible.

She/Her	1 Kid	Single	White

TL;DR: You don't have to set up an elaborate language-building routine to jumpstart your baby's vocabulary. Verbally engaging them in the things you do and observe every day will open them up to the world of conversation.

Every parent awaits the day their precious baby utters their first words—whose name will it be? You wonder if there is something you have to do to ensure your child will be verbal enough. The internet says do this; your parent group friends say do that; and then, of course, Aunt Betty's sister's cousin says, "You *must* do this. It is the only right way!"

The endless advice can make your head spin, and all you can think is, *I want to do everything for my baby, but I'm tired and not sure who to listen to or how to do it all perfectly.*

Well, I'm here to tell you there is no perfect way, and there isn't one right way. However, there *are* some stress-free ways to model language in your everyday routines. Research has shown the more language a child is exposed to when they are infants, the more likely they will be able to develop vocabulary, comprehension of written and spoken words, and engage in conversation to have their needs met.[1] The quality of the words you expose your baby to is as important as the amount. Aim to use full sentences and rich vocabulary as often as possible, while, of course, still using whatever love language feels most comfortable to you.

But even before you worry about your baby having a Webster's-size vocabulary, you can show your baby communicating is fun by making silly noises and faces at them and by imitating their own silly noises. These back-and-forth exchanges with your baby gets them ready to try to imitate your words one day!

Children find comfort in the sound of their parents and caretakers' voices. Here are some of the joyful ways I had fun modeling language for my own child each day:

- Making up silly rhymes while changing her diapers. ("Teddy bear has brown hair.")
- Carrying her in a baby carrier and describing what I was doing while shopping for food or folding laundry. ("This is your pink hat and your flower shirt!")
- Narrating whatever she was doing during tummy time and in the bath. ("Duck is yellow. You have ten toes.")

I hope you find times during the day where you remember to think out loud. You'll be a great language model for your child and further strengthen your loving bond!

"The quality of the words you expose your baby to is as important as the amount."

[1]Meredith L. Rowe, "A Longitudinal Investigation of the Role of Quantity and Quality of Child-Directed Speech in Vocabulary Development," *Child Development* 83, no. 5 (June 20, 2012): pp. 1762-1774, https://doi.org/10.1111/j.1467-8624.2012.01805.x.

Chapter 35

A DOCTOR'S NOTE.

Guidance on baby holding, bathing, preparedness in the home, and routine check-ups.

Dr. Raphael Sharon is a general pediatrician with a special interest in Autism Spectrum Disorder. He resides in Edmonton, Alberta, Canada, with his wife, Devra, their five kids, and their Bernedoodle named Lucky. He is the current Chair for the Action Committee for Children and Teens of the Canadian Pediatric Society and is also Director for Alberta and Northwest Territories of the Canadian Pediatric Society. He is a clinical associate professor in the department of pediatrics at the University of Alberta.

He/Him	5 Kids	Married

TL;DR: As a new parent, there's so much to learn before you find your groove, and it takes a lot of practice and a few panicked phone calls to your pediatrician. Thankfully, that's what they're there for! It's okay to seek guidance when going through the journey of your baby's first stages of development.

When you have your first baby, things are exciting and scary at the same time—mixed emotions are common and natural to have as a parent.

In my practice, I see lots of newborn babies every day. I love my job, and holding babies every day gives me so much joy. Holding a baby comes very naturally to me now because I've done it a lot, both as a father and as a pediatrician. It takes a little practice, however the transition from awkward to second nature will happen for you too, and quicker than you might think.

In your arms—tips and best practices for optimal baby-holding

Right after they are born, the baby's neck muscles and motor skills—the body's ability to manage the process of movement—are still weak and need to develop more. You can help the baby with that development in the way you hold them.

Always make sure to support your newborn's head and neck when holding them. There are a few ways of holding the baby that I like best.

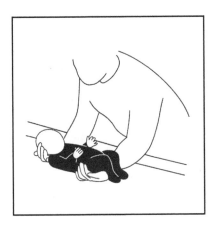

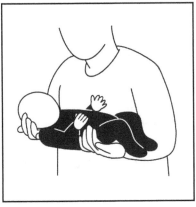

• When they're lying down, slide one hand under their head and neck, put your other hand under their bottom, and gently scoop them up close to your chest.

Illustrations by Gabby Nguyen

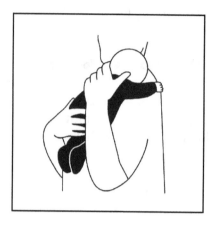

• You can also hold your baby against your chest with their head a little over your shoulder. Support their head and neck with one hand and hold their bum with the other.

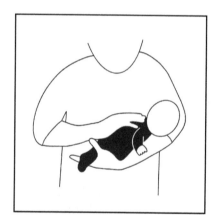

• Laying your baby tummy down and cradled along the length of your arm or your belly, facing out, can be calming and soothing to you and your child.

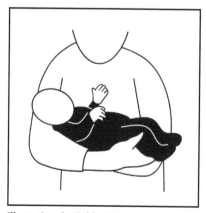

• Using the cradle hold with the baby's head in the crook of your arm allows you to look at your baby. This is wonderful for your interactions—you can smile and talk to your baby.

Illustrations by Gabby Nguyen

Always support your baby's head for the first four months. By about one month, your baby may be able to lift their head off a surface. Around four months, they should be able to hold their head up when placed in a supported seated position. Of course, never leave your baby unattended.

When holding your baby or wearing them in a carrier, make sure to do so safely. Do not hold your baby near hot food, beverages, or cooking surfaces that could burn them.

Friends and family love holding babies too. When a child or an elderly person wants to hold your baby, you can help them do so safely by asking them to sit down in a sturdy chair or on the floor. Then, gently place your baby in their cradled arms. Keep a careful watch, and do not leave the baby.

Back to sleep, tummy to play
To keep your baby safe and to help prevent SIDS (Sudden Infant Death Syndrome), or "crib death," pediatricians recommend your baby sleep on their back (not their tummy). It is also recommended to have your baby sleep in your bedroom (but *not* in your bed) for the first six to twelve months.

Keep soft objects out of the crib (including pillows, toys, bumper pads, etc.) to keep your baby safe inside their crib. Your baby in a warm onesie or sleeper should be the only thing in the crib.

Make sure your crib follows the standards of your government body, and if you don't know, check. In the United States, the best source of this information is the Consumer Product Safety Commission. You can find them at cpsc.gov. In Canada, Health Canada is the regulatory body. You can find them at canada.ca/en/health-canada.

I encourage tummy time during the day to help strengthen your baby's neck muscles and motor skills. To do this, when they are alert and well-rested, place your baby on their tummy on a safe, flat surface. Baby's head should be positioned to the left or right side for breathing. As they are able to, they will lift their head briefly, and then lay it back down. As they grow stronger, they will be able to hold their head up for longer periods.

Aim to do this three to four times a day for about four to five minutes at a time. Stay with your baby during this exercise for safety. It can be a truly wonderful time to interact. If your baby is not interested or dislikes this exercise, try it at another time of the day, or in a different environment. If they still don't like it, it's okay; keep trying in various safe spaces.

Just remember this golden rule: put your baby on their back to sleep and their tummy to play.

Splish-splash in the bath

Wait for the umbilical cord stump to fall off before you give your baby their first bath. Until that time, you can sponge bathe them.

To give a sponge bath, work in a warm, well-lit area where your baby is safe and never left alone. Use two washcloths. Dip the first washcloth in warm water and use a small amount of baby-safe soap. Wash the baby in small areas at a time, such as the foot and leg, then use the second washcloth and warm, clean water to rinse. If the baby gets a little fussy or cold, cover the area you've just washed with a dry towel as you move to the next area.

Gently wash your baby's vagina or penis with soap and water, and rinse with water. The foreskin of uncircumcised penises should not be pulled back in the first year of life.

Once you do give them a bath, use a baby tub until they're able to sit capably on their own.

Fill the baby tub with about two to three inches of water and make sure to test the temperature of the water with the inside of your wrist. Gently lower your baby's bottom into the baby tub and let them splash around a bit while you have a hold on them. You can use a washcloth to gently wash them.

A Doctor's Note.

Always make sure to stay within arm's reach of your baby and never leave them unattended.

You can start using the family tub when your baby is able to sit on their own, typically around 6 months. A child can be seriously injured or die if they are left alone in the tub at this age. Never leave the bathroom, become distracted, or use a hairdryer or any powered device while your child is in the tub. Find a way to be comfortable on the floor, or use a low stool to remain beside them alert and focused for the entire bath.

You can incorporate bathing as part of your baby's bedtime routine, and it's a nice time to bond and relax together. Eventually, the routine will help signal to your baby that the next thing on the schedule is reading a bedtime story and going to sleep.

Help: my baby is mobile now

When babies are newborns, parents often can't wait for them to start walking and talking. But once they become mobile, baby proofing becomes a top priority. Babies start to crawl around nine months. It's a lot of fun to watch them go from one end of your living room to the other, and you should encourage that mobility.

Here are some safety precautions to think about once your little one gets more mobile:

- Remove small objects from the floor your baby could put in their mouth.
- Keep all cabinets locked with a baby lock.
- Never leave cleaning supplies or buckets full of water or soap unattended. A child can drown in a very small amount of water.
- Detergent pods for clothes and dishes are attractive to babies and toddlers and very dangerous if ingested. Keep them in a locked cabinet.
- Put the mattress of your crib on the lowest setting once they start crawling, as they often start pulling themselves up to stand as they become more mobile.

- Be especially cautious of items with small-button batteries (remote controls, games, toys, flameless candles) as accidental ingestion could be life-threatening.
- Be sure all open electrical outlets are covered and that electrical cords are not within your baby's reach.

Keep up with your pediatrician

It's important to visit your pediatrician at your regularly scheduled appointments. Typically we see children at birth, then at one, two, four, six, nine, twelve, and eighteen months. Then annually from age two years on, just like you. A pediatrician will help keep track of your child's health, growth, and development. We will perform physical exams, diagnose and treat any problems that may arise, as well as provide education and advice.

Pediatricians will also provide anticipatory guidance and parenting information, and answer any questions you may have about your baby's health and development.

Immunizations provide many health benefits and pediatricians want to ensure your child can benefit from these as well. The recommended schedule of immunizations has been researched *extensively*. It is documented to be the safest and most effective method to protect children from the effects of vaccine-preventable infectious diseases.

Vaccines are carefully timed to provide protection when kids are most vulnerable and will provide the strongest response from your kid's immune system when given according to schedule.

As you go through the journey of your baby's first stages of development, at times, it may feel like you're in that phase for so long. But I promise, it goes by in the blink of an eye. Cherish every moment—before you know it, they'll be off on their own.

"Just remember this golden rule: put your baby on their back to sleep and their tummy to play."

Chapter 36

FEEDING TWINS.

Work with what you've got.

Ashley Countryman (she/her) is a mother, wife, and friend to all. She is passionate about human connections and inclusivity. While her studies and passion were in early childhood development, her career took off in design. Most days, you can find Ashley laughing with her family and enjoying music, food, DIY projects, or spontaneous trips to the mountains or beach.

She/Her	2 Kids	Woman	Gay

TL;DR: Feeding twins is no easy feat. However, streamlining the feeding (and clean-up) process and owning the feeding decisions that work best for you will allow you to be present with your babies instead of focused on the logistics.

Parenting twins is double the action, double the fun, and double the overwhelming feeling of what-in-the-world-did-I-just-step-into. Don't deny yourself the luxury of knowing we all feel this way in the throes of parenting twins.

My advice to you: scrap all those first-time parent ideals and just work with what you've got! Continually remind yourself to plan ahead, prioritize on the fly, and change the plan when you need to. That's the new plan.

Naturally, the first big hurdle is feeding. It varies with each baby and family, so be ready to make adjustments that work for you. I had a limited ability to breastfeed, so after about a month, I decided to switch to formula. It wasn't my first choice, but our priority was increasing the twins' weight, so we did what we had to do. Thanks to formula, we continued to host their private dining parties every three hours.

Feeding twins is a *process*. The goal is to streamline so that all feeding (and clean-up) supplies are at your fingertips. I decided to buy as many bottles as there were feedings per baby—sixteen total. I used my kitchen for prep and turned my dining room table into a command center with burp rags, a basket for bibs, diapers, wipes, and all other baby needs.

I set up shop as if I were a café barista prepping for the morning rush. Having everything measured and ready to go beforehand meant I could focus on my kids rather than the logistics when it was feeding time. Streamlining the feeding process not only helped my babies grow strong, but it gave me the space to recover from labor and delivery and grow stronger as a parent. Here are some tips that may help you with feeding twins efficiently:

Set a timer for yourself. Even though you want as much sleep as possible, try to wake up ten minutes before feeding time. A little time to wake up and center yourself allows you to be more present and endure those long days and nights when all the feedings start to run together.

Prepare a command center in a few different places around your home. I recommend including an extra bodysuit, burp rag, pacifier, wipes, chapstick, water or cup, book, and an alarm. Don't forget to add a little treat for yourself—something that gives you the tiniest moment of dopamine, like a piece of chocolate or some dried fruit. Between lack of sleep and healing from delivery, having that little treat tricked my brain to get in gear for the next alarm three hours later.

Remember, the days may seem long, but the years go by fast. You won't remember the prep work, but you will remember the moments it buys you with your babies.

Chapter 37

BREASTFEEDING.

To breastfeed or not to breastfeed? Here's some advice from someone who did it both ways.

Marie Rocha is a Black early-stage investor and mom of Kayla and Aidan. She lives in Connecticut and is very passionate about helping founders.

She/Her	2 Kids	Heterosexual	Black

TL;DR: Breastfeeding may work well for one baby and not another, and that is not a failure of your body. What's important is that your baby gets the nourishment they need, and there are many ways to accomplish this.

With all the nutritional benefits and antibodies, moms should breastfeed their babies, right? That's how I felt when my first child was born. At the slightest whimper, she would latch on like a suction cup. Just excellent parenting, I figured.

Fast-forward five years to the arrival of my second child. Now a veteran, I assumed it would be easy.

Unfortunately, his delivery came with a big slice of humble pie. Breastfeeding was a disaster! My ducts refused to cooperate. I begged, drank concoctions with milk thistle, among other less appetizing smoothies. I worked with a lactation specialist, all to no avail.

I was not prepared for how difficult it would be to breastfeed my son. There were many tears and frustrations from both of us. Finally, after four months of stress and feeling like I had failed him, I decided to stop breastfeeding altogether and started him on formula. In hindsight, it was the best decision I could have made.

Looking back on my two wildly different experiences, here's the advice I wish someone had given me about breastfeeding:

Be mentally prepared for things not to go exactly as planned.

Prepare for engorged breasts and cracked and/or sore nipples. Tip: compresses, creams, and warm showers help.

Don't be afraid to ask for help.

The first two to three days are more challenging because the process is new to you and you're learning. Don't be bashful about asking for help on technique, especially while at the hospital.

Breast pads are not gimmicks.

Be prepared for at least one wet T-shirt moment. Mine happened on the first postpartum date with my partner. My shirt was soaked with breast milk! Keep breast pads nearby at all times.

Celebrate all wins—small and large alike.

Celebrate two-week or two-year breastfeeding milestones. And if you aren't breastfeeding, remember breast milk alternatives have nourished kids for decades. Celebrate that provision as well!

Expect lots of unsolicited advice. Take it all with a grain of salt. (Yes, including mine.)

I was encouraged to create my own organic baby formula. A well-intentioned idea I attempted but probably shouldn't have.

Most importantly, give yourself a break!

Embrace all the options available to parents and babies.

Thirteen years later, I dare you to distinguish which of my two wonderful teens was breastfed for a year and a half and which I struggled to breastfeed for four months.

Take a stretch break.

Chapter 38

TUMMY TIME.

Getting through this tricky milestone will set the path for crawling—no pressure.

Lindsey Lewis was born in New Mexico and is a proud Tigua Indian, Hispanic woman. She is a single mother to two fierce daughters, Evelyn (5) and Teagan (4). Lindsey enjoys reading, making dream catchers, and playing games with her kids.

She/Her	2 Kids	Bisexual	Indigenous Native American

TL;DR: Tummy time builds motor function and muscles babies need to crawl. So don't panic; get creative.

Helping your baby reach important milestones like crawling presents its own set of triumphs and anxieties. For me, the tummy-time stage for my first baby was interrupted by pregnancy with my second. Talk about a tummy challenge! Unexpected pregnancy presented a layer of difficulty to new motherhood, particularly when encouraging my first-born baby to crawl.

Tummy time not only helps you bond with your baby but encourages them to crawl. So, when supporting them during tummy time, get creative and stay determined. Ease their fears by letting them play and explore.

If you feel like you're failing at tummy time for any reason, these tried-and-true tips might help.

- Pick out your baby's favorite toys to entice them to crawl. At first, this will encourage them to lift up enough to get the toy. And eventually, your little one will try to wiggle their way to it.
- Your support and presence can prompt your baby to try and reach you. Have fun! You can make funny faces, sing songs, and do silly dances.
- A change of scenery can be refreshing. Change up the room or go to an entirely different location. This switch-up may help keep your baby engaged.
- If your baby starts to cry during tummy time, try to soothe them with back rubs and a calming song. Then, try again. The goal is to stay in tummy time longer and longer over time.

These tricks helped my baby eventually enjoy tummy time, which made it easier for both of us. I was thrilled when she started crawling—backward! Still counts.

Encouraging babies to stay in tummy time longer will help them crawl sooner. But, most importantly, enjoy this time with your little one. Follow their cues and always be willing to try again.

"When supporting your baby during tummy time, get creative and stay determined."

Chapter 39

WATCHING TV.

How to watch TV without ruining your baby.

Dr. Michele Foss-Snowden, PhD, is a professor of communication studies and the voice behind the podcast *The TV Doctor*. She lives in Sacramento, California, with her husband and daughter. They're all probably watching *Star Trek* right now.

She/Her	1 Kid	Married

TL;DR: Whether you're watching the latest episode of your favorite show or listening to Mozart compositions, how you engage with the arts matters just as much as how often.

I felt the blood drain from my face as I heard my daughter's pediatrician say, "We recommend that children under the age of two not watch TV."

I looked down at my sweet baby and experienced a wave of guilt so heavy I was sure everyone in the room felt it. Just how badly had my binge-watching habit harmed her?

Here was my trusted doctor, telling me that, like cleaning products and uncovered swimming pools, I would have to keep my girl away from screens. I certainly had not been doing that.

An important note: I'm a professor of communication. I teach television. Watching TV is literally my job.

The doctor noticed my discomfort. "Here's the thing," she said. "We want babies to interact with real people, not just people on a screen."

I flew into defensive mode. My voice cracking, I said, "Oh, she interacts with me all day, even while we're watching TV! We treat TV like art! We dance to the theme songs. I explain to her what's happening. I mute the TV and read the captions when she's napping or while I breastfeed her. We watch shows about puppies and pyramids and...*Star Trek*! We watch *Star Trek*! I'm pretty sure she loves it!"

The doctor put her hand on my shoulder. "It sounds like you're doing fine. You're being thoughtful about it. That's important."

What she meant, and what all new parents today should know, is that TV and any form of creative arts *can* be bad depending on how you engage with it.

Art should be a tool to engage, not disconnect. So, we can mindfully help our babies enjoy art—even if it's a fictionalized TV show about alien planets.

Yes, my daughter watches more TV than is recommended by pediatricians. But how she watches matters. And I trust myself to make the right call for my kid.

So should you.

"Art should be a tool to engage, not disconnect."

Chapter 40

MILESTONES.

From crawling to standing to taking steps—how I learned to approach milestones as a way to connect with my unique kiddo.

Suzy Ultman grew-up in a tight-knit family of sisters playing, creating, dancing, and all-around mischief-making. When Suzy started her own family, she instilled the same sense of play and curiosity into her little boys. Moving from Portland to Amsterdam to Massachusetts, they found adventure and expanded their community. Over the years, their family changed shape and size, eventually becoming a blended family. Suzy is now nested with her husband and three sons in Ohio.

She/Her	4 Kids	Married	Blended Family

TL;DR: Child development milestones signal a deeper understanding of the uniqueness of your kiddo. Use them as a guidepost, not a caution sign.

My son, Oz, is big now—a young adult. Like all of us, there's still growth to be made, but I can look back and say with a smile, "Wow, we did it! He's on his path. He's him."

I didn't always know we'd get to this point. I had days that were really hard. I felt lost. I cried.

But then, when Oz was around three months old, and I finally started getting some sleep, I became completely captivated by this little being. He was chunky and smiley with hair that stood out like he was touching one of those static electricity generator balls. At six months, Oz began pulling himself around the room like a one-armed snake (the pediatrician called it "the army crawl").

Milestones.

Then, Oz went straight from pulling to standing, bypassing crawling.

My parenting books described missing the crawling milestone as problematic, and the pediatrician noted the same concern. I was nervous. What did this mean? There were some general questions on the matter: Was his brain missing a step? Would his brain miss other steps? Since I couldn't get any clear answers, I decided to enjoy each day with Oz and to set aside my worries about reaching milestones. Between doctor appointments, I tried my best to focus on the joy I felt watching his little life unfold.

As Oz developed, what came to light was an Autism Spectrum Disorder (ASD) diagnosis. The milestones along the way did indeed lead us to a new understanding of Oz's world. Interestingly enough, the milestones were just guideposts—they were simply Oz becoming Oz.

As I parented, I learned I was growing *with* Oz, side by side. Every milestone that was new for him was new for me too. Along the way, I discovered who he was and how he processed the world. I was learning how to guide him, assist him, and support him. And I was learning something else too—there isn't just one way to walk through this world. Through the ups and downs, we found our happy and celebrated by creating our own milestones!

Chapter 41

BABY'S FIRST NIGHT ON THEIR OWN.

When bedtime feels like mission impossible.

Bryan Wolf is a finance guy and Oregon native, born and raised. He is dad to Emma (26) and Jake (23), husband to Maureen, and in his free time enjoys running and rockhounding in the beautiful Pacific Northwest.

He/Him	2 Kids	Married	White

TL;DR: Letting your baby cry it out can be the hardest thing to do in the moment, but it's healthy and natural, and no, you're not a terrible parent for choosing this route.

Let's set the scene:

I'm sitting in the living room with my wife, pretending to watch TV, listening to my baby's blood-curdling screams coming from her room, and a wave of fears flash through my mind:

Can she breathe?

Is she going to fall out of the crib and hurt herself?

And loudest of all: Am I a terrible parent?

About a month after Emma was born, she was sleeping (mostly) through the night, and we were ready to transition her into her own room. The plan for that evening was simple:

Baby's First Night On Their Own.

Place the baby in the crib. (Check.)
Say some soothing words until baby is sleepy. (Check.)

Quietly leave the room. (Critical mission error.)

The moment we stepped out of the room, Emma began to cry. And cry. And cry. At first, it was just a bit of wailing, but it quickly crescendoed to the most horrific screams imaginable.

By this time I had stopped pretend-watching TV and was standing just outside her room with a flurry of panicked questions swirling through my brain, and I'm torn. This next step is important for babies' (and parents') development, but how can I stand here and listen to her cry so persistently?

So how did I get through it? Super Stealthy Dad Mode.

Goal: I won't let her see me, thus starting the bedtime process all over again, but I'll verify that she *is* getting enough oxygen in her lungs.

I re-enter her room, crawling so as not to draw attention to my presence. I lay on the floor by the crib, and wait. And after a surprisingly short amount of time, all crying ceased.

I slowly poked my head above the crib and there she was, eyes closed, breathing softly—a remarkably peaceful contrast to the wailing little being occupying the crib just minutes before. That being said, I still slept next to her crib that night (just in case).

Gut-wrenching, heartbreaking shrieks and tears: in the moment, you doubt your ability as a parent. But whether you let your baby self-soothe or step in when the crying starts, either method is healthy for your child's development.[1] So remember:

They can breathe. They will be okay. You are a good and loving parent, period.

[1]Harriet Hiscock et al., "Five-Year Follow-up of Harms and Benefits of BEHAVIORAL Infant Sleep INTERVENTION: Randomized Trial," *PEDIATRICS* 130, no. 4 (October 2012), https://doi.org/10.1542/peds.2011-3467.

Chapter 42

GUT HEALTH.

A practical approach to early gut health.

Dr. Tasneem Bhatia ("Dr. Taz") is an integrative health expert and the founder of CentreSpring MD. When not caring for patients as their holistic doctor, Dr. Taz can be found in Atlanta spending time with her husband and two young children reading, studying, practicing yoga, trying new things in the kitchen, and traveling.

| 2 Kids | Female | Indian |

TL;DR: Many newborn babies have some element of gut deficiency or unhealthy gut microbial balance, which leaves many first-time parents perplexed. Don't fret! You can create a foundation for a healthy gut by following some simple principles.

There are so many things to think about when a newborn arrives. I can reflect back on my days as an expectant new mom when it was all about the nursery, the gear, the pictures—never putting much thought into my gut health. In hindsight, I wish I knew then what I know now, since navigating gut health became a challenge for my son.

Understanding gut health and its implications for your newborn and their long-term health has only become more crucial to me with time—my son is now 12! Setting a foundation for a healthy gut should be as important as planning to breastfeed or use formula, picking out the new gear, or choosing nursery colors. Today, it is estimated that almost 90% of babies have some element of newborn gut deficiency or unhealthy gut-microbial balance.[1]

Gut Health.

Here is a quick teaching on the fundamentals of gut health: Starting as early as preconception, the gut microbiome, or the millions of bacteria that live in our gut, is forming in utero and passes to our unborn babies. The mother's nutrition, environmental burdens, and stress all influence this microbiome. As our babies pass through the birth canal, the mother's microbiome further influences the newborn's gut bacteria.

Gut bacteria influence the immune system, inflammatory response, metabolism, and even brain health. Research continues to emphasize what older systems of medicine, including Chinese and Ayurvedic medicine, already knew—that the gut really is ground zero for our health.

Early steps to create a gut health foundation for your child include maintaining your own healthy diet, lowering consumption of inflammatory foods and sugar, and preparing for breastfeeding for parents who go this feeding route. Breast milk has the ideal fat-to-protein ratio and also has prebiotics to help support the baby's microbiome, reducing the bad bacteria that trigger many of the illnesses we see today. I encourage mothers to think about their own diet—adding in healthy fats including nut butters, ghee, avocados, and olive oil. Bone broth and soups from bones are mainstays in Chinese medicine and Ayurvedic medicine for nursing moms, as these proteins help heal the gut and encourage healthy microbial balance.

But even breastfed babies are often partially formula-fed, so understanding what to look for in a formula is important as well. Formulas that have prebiotics and higher lipid levels can mimic the gut-protective effect of lowering bad bacteria and keeping the gut healthy.

As children transition away from exclusive breast or formula feeding, adding in a variety of foods that contain fiber becomes the next critical step in improving the gut microbiome. Fiber improves the pH of stool, which improves digestion and lowers the incidence of many atopic illnesses seen in the first year of life, including eczema, allergies, or reactive airways. Helping our children develop the palate for higher-fiber foods—fruits and vegetables without added sugars or sweeteners—is an important early step in establishing a healthy gut.

Inulin, a prebiotic that promotes the growth of healthy bacteria, also improves the population of bifidobacteria, a healthy bacteria that supports the gut, cognitive development, and immune function. Natural sources of inulin include bananas, chicory root, asparagus, and leeks—foods that babies can eat when properly prepared after eight months of age. Additionally, inulin supplementation has proven to be helpful in keeping stools consistently soft, formed, and properly influencing healthy gut bacteria.

Probiotic supplementation for both mom and baby is also recommended for babies who show classic digestive distress—constipation, skin rashes, gas, bloating, and colic. Adding in probiotics that contain bifidobacterium and lactobacillus bacteria are helpful in restoring a healthy infant gut and are now more widely available. **It is important to note that any supplementation should be cleared by your baby's doctor.**

It is possible to create a foundation for a healthy gut following the principles above and recognizing the warning signs of gut trouble. With a few of these dietary tweaks and actively thinking about probiotics, prebiotics, and inulin, you can create a healthy gut for your child and set them up for long-term health.

[1]Giorgio Casaburi et al., "Metagenomic Insights of the Infant Microbiome Community Structure and Function across Multiple Sites in the United States," Scientific Reports 11, no. 1 (January 21, 2021), https://doi.org/10.1038/s41598-020-80583-9.

"Setting a foundation for a healthy gut should be as important as planning to breastfeed or use formula, picking out the new gear, or choosing nursery colors."

Chapter 43

BREAST MILK BANKS.

When breast milk is best—and borrowed.

Alisa Norman and her husband of thirteen years are raising a ten-year-old and a three-year-old. She is a writer and a published author who was born and raised in Newark, New Jersey. Alisa loves to cook and create recipes. She also enjoys reading, music, boxing, and long drives with scenic views.

She/Her	2 Kids	Married	Black

TL;DR: Facing lactation issues is a profoundly personal and humbling experience for new birthing parents. One solution for these issues is utilizing a breast milk bank. Once you get past the emotional challenge of acceptance, you will find a wonderful, life-giving gift and a community of support.

My firstborn was a preemie who entered the world at just under twenty-six weeks and weighed a pound and a half. Throughout my pregnancy, I suffered from Hyperemesis Gravidarum, which is extreme, persistent nausea and vomiting during pregnancy that led to severe dehydration and disabled my breast milk production.

After two days of failed attempts to produce breast milk for my baby, the head neonatologist came into my room to drop a massive mom-bomb on me. She asked for my authorization to provide my newborn with milk from a breast milk bank.

She said, "This is critical for your baby's life, survival, development, and growth."

Breast Milk Banks.

Within a fraction of a millisecond, I thought, My baby needs breast milk for a chance at life, and I can't provide it! I felt lost and useless, as if I had been stripped of my motherhood, and was fighting the instinctive yearning to provide for my baby on my own. But I had to let all those thoughts and feelings go. My baby needed breast milk by any means necessary.

I decided to talk to the other mothers in the neonatal intensive care unit—the NICU. I asked them questions and listened to their stories. I stayed open and expressed how I felt. Deciding to connect with others who shared my experience allowed me to look beyond the discomfort and realize I was not alone. I entered a community of support and communication with the other mothers and I found much-needed connection. We were seen, heard, and understood.

More importantly, I watched my baby flourish and make daily progress, and I learned a lot about how breast milk banks work. For example, all breast milk donors go through rigorous medical testing and screening before they can donate. Once the donation is accepted, the breast milk itself is tested then pasteurized.

I am not the first nor will I be the last parent to feed my baby using a breast milk bank. As new parents, we should not be afraid of seeking connection with others and tapping into the resources available to us—this is how we learn, grow, and help.

I'm exceedingly grateful to all those selfless, caring women who choose compassion and community by donating their breast milk to babies whose survival depends on it. To all the parents facing this choice: breast bank milk does not make you any less of a provider. You are loving, caring for, and raising a little human. That is empowering and powerful.

And you can take that to the bank.

"My baby needed breast milk by any means necessary."

Chapter 44

POOP!

Yup, poop.

Jay Leary is a technologist, creator of a parenting advice website, and the father of two delightful young ladies who occasionally let him sleep through the night.

He/Him	2 Kids	Married

TL;DR: Everybody poops, but baby poop is in a category all its own. It's normal to see all kinds and lots of it. Be on the lookout for white, gray, or bloody poop, which means call the doctor. And always have wipes at the ready.

Take a second to picture a poop. You know what? I bet we're picturing the same thing. Our mental construct of the stuff is rock solid. Poop is an emoji for Pete's sake.

Now take that construct and shelve it.

Your baby's poop will not look like an emoji. It will not look like the poop you pictured. At least in the beginning, it will be something fantastically different that will challenge your perceptions of #2.

The first stool you'll encounter is called meconium. It only lasts a few days and is basically the aftermath of all the things your baby consumed in the womb. Meconium is dark-ish green, sticky, and exceptionally weird.

Once your child really dives into breast milk or formula, you're in for a fun ride. You'll encounter vibrant yellows, tans, and greens—amazingly technicolor stuff. You might see little curds or seeds and pasty streaks. And you know what's crazy? It doesn't really smell that bad. I mean...I'm not saying it smells good, but it's not what you'd expect.

In the beginning babies might poop after every feeding (which is a lot of poops). As they get closer to two months, the frequency will probably slow down, but you won't see big kid poops until they start eating solid food.

Of course, there are things to watch out for. White or gray poops deserve a call to the doctor's office. Any hint of blood needs attention. Excessively hard poops could indicate dehydration or illness. Really loose or more frequent movements could suggest diarrhea.

As always, keep an eye on things and talk to your pediatrician if something seems off.

But take this to heart: the poop you know so well is decidedly not the poop you'll encounter. Welcome, friends, to your next digestive adventure.

"Your baby's poop will not look like an emoji."

Chapter 45

NEWBORN ESSENTIALS.

Focusing on the basics is better for you, your baby, and your wallet!

Sarah Gould Steinhardt (she/her) and **Juliet Fuisz** (she/her) are the cofounders of Welcome Baby USA, a nonprofit organization that provides struggling families with the essential care items their newborn will need in their first month of life. Since 2018, they've served thousands of families from coast to coast. Juliet resides in Ohio with her daughter, twin sons, and husband; Sarah resides in New York with her two sons, stepdaughter, and husband.

Each Have 3 Kids	Each Are Married

TL;DR: It can be easy to become immediately overwhelmed by the growing list of things a newborn baby needs. Relieve some of that anxiety with this list of essential, cost-effective items to get you through that first hectic month.

As you wait for your little one to arrive, the list of items you think you'll need to care for your baby may seem to grow longer by the day. It's so easy—and understandable—to feel overwhelmed by the advice and recommendations coming from friends, family, and social media.

We are here to tell you that the list can actually be quite short, and your baby definitely doesn't need to break the bank.

As moms and cofounders of a nonprofit that gives struggling families a comprehensive package containing all the essentials a newborn needs in their first month of life, we believe there is a universal set of basic items every baby needs to thrive. Our knowledge comes from firsthand experience (with six kids between the two of us) and through lots of research and feedback from the thousands of families we have served.

The most obvious things you'll need for your baby aside from a **safe place to sleep** and **nourishment** are **diapers and wipes**. If your baby is born full-term, we recommend diapers in both newborn size and size 1. Purchasing in bulk will save a significant amount of money. For families who don't have a stable address or income, finding your local diaper bank and obtaining about 220 diapers can sustain your baby comfortably through the first month. **Rash creams** will prevent and treat skin irritations that can be painful and distressing for parents and babies. A gentle **baby wash** will also help keep your baby clean and comfortable during bath time.

In addition to a **car seat**, an inexpensive **baby carrier** can help you get around by foot or public transportation. An infant **grooming kit** that includes a **thermometer** and other newborn-specific items can relieve a number of early concerns. **Bottles** (for either breast milk or formula—you'll need to choose the **nipples** that are right for each) are a necessity, and **pacifiers** can be a lifesaver when your little one is extra fussy.

When it comes to clothes, we believe less is more. About half a dozen **onesies**, some **footed pajamas**, a couple of **swaddle blankets**, and several pairs of **socks**, **mittens**, and **hats** are all your baby needs.

Having these supplies on hand when you come home with your baby will provide a sense of calm and confidence. Every parent and baby deserves to have these basic, essential items within arm's reach during those vulnerable and sleepless first few weeks together. We hope that as you begin your parenting journey you can take comfort in knowing that oftentimes, less is more.

Chapter 46

NIGHTTIME ROUTINE.

Five things I've learned.

Nabil Zerizef and his wife, Courtney (she/her), have been married for thirteen years. They became parents through adopting their son, Adi, at birth, who is now three years old (love to his birth mom, Ammu). Nabil is a middle school principal who is learning to intentionally balance work life and family time.

He/Him	1 Kid	Married	Arab American

TL;DR: In the busyness of life, establishing consistency can be hard. However, committing to a few routines (even imperfectly) will allow your little one predictability and you a chance to prioritize special moments together.

Growing up, I remember when my mother was working four jobs, including nights and weekends. Settling into a routine was not always easy. Now that my wife and I are both working parents, we face a similar challenge. We both want to be able to work and also spend as much time with our son, Adi, as possible. Establishing routines (especially those around nighttime) have helped us make the most of the time we do have.

Believe me, our family's routines are still far from perfect because we all have our own challenging situations, but the reality is that kids respond best to consistent and predictable environments. So here are some things we did (that you can do) to create manageable nighttime routines.

Nighttime Routine.

Decide on needs and values. My wife and I have had many conversations about our needs as parents and as a family. We talked about how those needs fit with what we value in life. For us, it came down to focusing on quality time with our son, sharing parental responsibilities, and still getting enough time to ourselves in the evening. Work emails can wait until after the baby has gone to bed, for example.

Find resources. Books (like this one!), technology, social media accounts, pediatricians, and good, old-fashioned conversations with others can be super helpful. We also keep an eye out for ways to make life easier, such as plates that suction to the table, having a video monitor in our son's room that connects to our phone, and pre-measuring formula into small containers.

Set a schedule. We decided on specific times for play, meals, baths, brushing teeth, diaper/pajamas, stories, nighttime songs, and transferring to the bed or crib. Important questions to consider are, Who is going to do each of these? How long will each likely take? My favorite bedtime tasks are to take Adi on a walk and to sing him songs in the rocking chair each night!

Be flexible. Even the best plans can fail. At our house, when things are just not going well for one reason or another, we call it a "B Day." We adjust, improvise, and become less rigid. If B days are happening too often, however, we know it's time to reexamine our original plan, maybe move things around a bit or try new activities.

Keep perspective. You know your baby best, and you know yourself even better. Everyone will want to have an opinion about what you "should do" when raising a child. Take that input (along with everything you just read) with a gigantic grain of salt. The first year is a learning year; you will quickly find what works and what doesn't. Trust your own instinct!

Nighttime routines are important, and in our family, we found that the routines we intentionally designed worked much better than those that happened by default. Put aside some time and plan it out to promote harmony for your newly expanded family.

Chapter 47

FEEDING YOUR BABY.

Flexibility and courage when feeding your child.

Rohit Goel (he/him) and **Ria Ghosh** (she/her) are an Indian immigrant family who moved to the US a few years ago. They live in the DMV area (DC, Maryland, Virginia) with their young son, who is also the first grandchild on both sides of the family.

1 Kid	Heterosexual	Married	Asian

TL;DR: If figuring out feeding feels tough in the beginning, don't stress. There are many options available and you will find what works best for you and your baby.

Feeding is a key aspect in the care of a newborn, and it's likely you may feel uncertainty and pressure about how to proceed. Their bodies aren't like yours yet, so you may have questions about the mechanics of breastfeeding or bottle feeding, when to feed, how much, and so on.

First, know whatever you're experiencing is natural and normal. This is one of those parenting topics that is rarely openly discussed, but it's nothing to feel shame about. Safe places to get more answers and ease some of your concern include lactation consultants, birthing nurses, and even online forums.

You will also realize that your body—and your little one's—will change significantly in the first few weeks. So if things are not going swimmingly in the beginning, know you are not alone. For us, we worked together and found our balance within a reasonable amount of time. Keep your chin up and keep at it.

When it comes to breast milk, a nursing body follows a supply-demand pattern. The more you nurse (or pump), the more your body will produce (to a reasonable point). If you reduce that time spent, your milk supply will also decrease over time.

If you have access to a hospital-grade pump, it is extremely useful because the strength of the suction is much better than most commercially-available pumps. They can be rented from medical supply companies. If that's not possible, don't be concerned—there are many good options available.

The reality is, you and your baby are figuring out what they need together. No matter which method you pursue, sometimes feeding may come naturally and other times, it may feel hard. Don't despair. You, along with every other parent who has been in your position before, will figure out a feeding rhythm that works; it can just take some time and patience.

Your newborn is highly dependent on you but is also your biggest ally. Babies are more resilient than we give them credit for, given how cute and fragile they appear. Your little one will absorb every ounce of energy they need (and they don't need all that much) from either breastfeeding or formula—whichever method you decide to use.

Trust your child and their instinct for how much they need, and be patient with yourself and your child through the trial-and-error process. Your baby will be strong regardless, and ultimately, all your worries will be nothing but memories.

"No matter which method you pursue, sometimes feeding may come naturally and other times, it may feel hard. Don't despair."

Chapter 48

THE PERFECT* DIAPER BAG.

(*Perfect for *you!*).

Doug Cornett is a teacher living in Cleveland, Ohio. He writes mystery books for kids (*Finally, Something Mysterious*, Knopf) and dedicates them to his wife, Anna, and their kids, Leo and Althea. He's still trying to remember to pack everything they need in the diaper bag before leaving the house.

He/Him	2 Kids	Married	Heterosexual

TL;DR: While there are some basic essentials that every baby needs, the "perfect diaper bag" doesn't exist! Learn the must-haves for your child, and take a quick check to make sure they are there every time you leave the house.

Before kids, I pictured a diaper bag as a cloth sack with a few diapers in it. A pack of wet wipes. A pacifier or two. Baby bottle. What else could you need?

Oh, the folly of my ways. Now I know that the diaper bag is your tool belt and your survival kit. It will become the most essential bag during the first few years of your kid's life.

Like most important things, I learned the importance of diaper bags the hard way.

When I took my son to his one-month doctor's appointment without an extra bottle of milk, I found out just how loud and long a nine-pound human can cry.

The Perfect* Diaper Bag.

When my son surprised my wife and me with a blowout of volcanic proportions at our favorite restaurant, I learned that an extra pair of clothes—for the baby and for you—are always a good idea.

And that roadside gas station bathroom taught me the value of a portable changing pad.

The truth is, there is no such thing as a perfect diaper bag because every kid and parent has different needs. Maybe, like us, a pair of EpiPens live in a side pocket. Or maybe you can't be caught anywhere without a certain stuffed giraffe. As your kid gets older, their needs evolve. But for an infant, here are some universal must-haves:

- Diapers. (Like a good party, the more the merrier.)
- Wet wipes. (Yep, they need to be wet. And a full pack—there's no worse feeling than pulling out the last wipe in the pack when you really need a whole lot more.)
- Burp cloths. (Otherwise, you'll be buying yourself a lot of new shirts.)
- Breast milk/formula bottles and granola bars (snacks for baby *and* for you).
- Skin protection. (i.e., diaper cream, baby sunblock—for when they are 6 months or older—sun hat, blanket, etc.)
- Changing pad. (Surfaces suddenly seem grosser when you're about to lay your baby on them.)
- Extra clothes. (This goes for you too—take it from a guy who's been peed on in public more than he'd like to admit.)
- Hand sanitizer.
- Extra masks for the grownups.
- Nose aspirator.
- Pacifiers.
- A small toy or two.

With your close-to-perfect diaper bag, you're ready to face the world. Just don't forget to bring the baby!

Chapter 49

CREATIVE INTERACTION.

We don't need to neglect our goals and tasks as parents in order to spend time with our baby.

Ahlam Soliman is a PhD student at Michigan State University. Ahlam is an Egyptian mother and wife. Her son, Malek, is nine years old. In addition to spending time with her son, Ahlam enjoys reading and listening to classical music in her free time (which is rare).

She/Her	1 Kid	Female	Middle Eastern

TL;DR: When you feel overwhelmed by your to-do list, screen time for your kid is an easy go-to while you get stuff done. But with a little advance thought and preparation, there are simple ways to engage kids creatively, support their development, and still accomplish your tasks—win-win-win!

When things feel overwhelming, screen time seems like the easiest way to keep kids occupied (and the convenience can be so welcome!). With the baby entertained, you can finish your other tasks like cooking, studying, or taking calls.

I was a stay-at-home mom during the first two years of my son's life, and at the same time, I was preparing for graduate school. I strived to find balance between caring for my son and achieving my plans.

I didn't think that screen time would be most conducive to my child's brain development, especially during early infancy. But the question remained: How do we creatively entertain and also fulfill our duties as parents?

After wrestling with this question, I can offer my perspective, which is by no means comprehensive. I hope it helps you envision ways to bolster your baby's development by engaging with other types of entertainment.

My goal was to create interactive activities to enhance his developmental milestones. For example, let's take language acquisition—a pivotal developmental process that prepares babies for their first words. Like any kid, my son would get bored after playing with his toys for a while. But what if I needed to study? This might sound odd, but I used to study out loud with him, pretending I was giving a lecture. I would do it in a playful way so that it was entertaining. He would listen and smile back at me. We interacted with one another, he internalized the language I used, and I got to finish studying; win-win-win!

Another thing I used to do when it was time to cook was to give Malek pans and spoons and have him sit in front of me. Then, I would start cooking and talk to him about the recipe I was making. Amazingly, he would mimic what I was doing joyfully. Another win-win activity!

Finding creative ways to engage with my son was not always easy, believe me. But taking the time to be creative allowed him to enjoy himself and grow healthily, and, just as important, I could finish my tasks and feel accomplished.

**"But the question remained:
How do we creatively entertain them
and also fulfill our duties as parents?"**

Chapter 50

SLEEP TRAINING.

For when you're examining (or reexamining) your baby's sleep options. How you feel about sleep training might change over time, and that's okay!

Natalie Willes is a Los Angeles native with Argentine and Russian roots who calls beautiful Portland, Oregon, home. Along with her kitty, Dennis, she shares her home with two kids and a spouse. After helping over ten thousand families around the world get their kids to sleep through the night and take healthy naps, she's learned a thing or two about the intense reality that is kids and sleep.

She/Her	2 Kids	Heterosexual	Hispanic

TL;DR: There are many opinions on how to help babies learn to sleep, and most of the time, those opinions are incredibly personal. Choosing to create healthy sleep habits starts with learning who your family is and what your baby needs.

For many families, sleep is unexpectedly hard and full of variables. Your first baby might sleep well while your second or third child struggles. You may find yourself looking at your peers' kids and wondering, What's wrong with me? Why can't I figure out how to get my baby to sleep? In addition, chronic lack of sleep will catch up to you and your family fast, making you feel overwhelmed and more exhausted than you thought possible.

It doesn't take long for a sleep-deprived parent to hit the internet looking for help, only to encounter a world they may have not been aware of until they had a baby. Some parents have strong feelings about sleep training, which is defined as teaching a child to be laid down awake, flat on their back in an empty crib. The goal of sleep training is for babies to go from being awake to asleep without help from a caretaker or sleep lovey. Newborns are universally assisted to sleep. So when it comes time for an older baby to learn to self-soothe to sleep, they typically resist.

Here's the thing: how parents think they feel about sleep training and what they'll be comfortable with implementing when the time comes can be very different. Some parents are more comfortable with the prospect of sleep training than they thought they'd be once they experience severe sleep deprivation. Others feel wholly against the concept no matter how sleep deprivation impacts them.

There is no lack of resources online for dealing with your baby's sleep issues. Look for an online course or trusted sleep coach who has good recommendations from other parents. Check local, city, and state programs for free or reduced-price classes or assistance. Having someone to answer your questions really does make the whole process easier.

What often surprises parents most about the sleep training process isn't the actual process itself, but rather the unsolicited comments from everyone around them. Even more surprising? You might consider yourself to be a nonjudgmental person, but you may find yourself thinking unkind things about a fellow parent who makes a different choice than you when it comes to their child's sleep.

Here is my biggest piece of advice as an experienced sleep coach—focus on your own family and don't worry about the choices your friends make. Be the supportive friend who says, "It's okay if we're doing things differently. I am right here next to you on this parenthood journey and I know we're both doing our best and trying to figure this out."

"There is no lack of resources online for dealing with your baby's sleep issues."

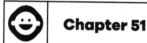

Chapter 51

BABYWEARING.

Babywearing allows for adventure and strengthens the bond with your baby.

Jeremy Daniel, his wife, Sagrario, and toddler, Hudson, are expecting their second child soon. They grow and learn together in Upper Manhattan, where they like to cycle, kayak, skateboard, and visit New York City parks. Now that they are almost a family of four, Jeremy can see that all the parenting cliches are true!

He/Him	2 Kids	Married	Caucasian

TL;DR: Baby's world is so small before they're mobile, but babywearing allows you to introduce them to their surroundings and bond along the way.

My son pointed his finger up into the air toward the sound that echoed around us. We were alone in the woods, Hudson facing outward from the babywearing belt around my waist. The steady drizzle of early spring rain dripped on our hats and the foliage around us. Up in a tree, a blue jay chirped as it flew out of its nest; Hudson giggled in delight and watched it fly to the ground for seed.

"That's a blue jay. See how brilliantly blue its wings are?" His wide eyes absorbed it all.

Babywearing opens up adventures to new worlds for both the baby and parent. When Hudson was an infant, I wore him facing me in what felt like a tiny cocoon. At this early stage, the purpose was to create warmth and protection from the elements as we moved from point A to point B. An ordinary trip to the grocery store could be an opportunity for us to feel connected inwardly; he'd hear my heartbeat and feel my breaths expand my stomach and chest upward.

For this position, it's important to see your infant's face and know it's free from obstruction. The chin should not be tucked as it can compress your little one's airway.

As Hudson grew bigger, I looked forward to the day I could baby-wear him facing outward. It was like a rite of passage—an expansion of our horizons together. When that day arrived, I had to remember to adjust the button on the carrier so the harness adequately supported his weight. Then, when he was fully strapped in with his body turned out toward the world, we could not contain our shared excitement.

The purpose had now changed from protection to exploration.

We took daily hikes through the woods in Inwood Hill Park in Manhattan and I would ruminate out loud about health and safety, politics, and the movements of insects. Hudson turned his head in every direction to point his gaze and his fingers at objects near and far. I followed his fingers and eyes: "That's a squirrel. See how it climbs up trees waving its bushy tail? And that's a bridge there in the distance. And see this wide river? It's named Hudson, just like you!"

Beyond the park hikes, babywearing also opened us up to new playgrounds around the city. We discovered vast sand pits in Central Park, a playground in Washington Heights with an intricate sprinkler system and an ice cream truck stationed nearby, and a place to practice climbing at the top of Fort Tryon Park.

Don't underestimate the inward and outward experience that can emerge when you take your baby along for the ride.

Enjoy your new adventure together!

"An ordinary trip to the grocery store could be an opportunity for us to feel connected inward-ly; he'd hear my heartbeat and feel my breaths expand my stomach and chest upward."

Chapter 52

THE CHANGING STATION.

Stay prepared for all the curveballs.

Kelly DeLucco is a professional baker and mother of two boys. She claims motherhood is the hardest role and biggest honor in life. She lives in Portland, Oregon, with her husband and sons.

She/Her	2 Kids	Married	Heterosexual

TL;DR: The changing station is sometimes a place of mystery—like the toilet will be later. While your baby is little, stay prepared for what's inside each diaper, and be ready to smile with your baby all the way until they are fresh and dry.

With our first son, the changing station was like command central. It had everything we needed and was our go-to for diaper changes.

With our second, we pretty quickly ditched the changing table and just used whatever surface we had around. Who has time to walk to the baby's room when the diapers, wipes, and couch are right here?

As my boy grew, so did his poop. And as practiced as I was, I was totally unprepared for his newfound fascination with it.

Changing diapers became a contortion sport. I'd have *his* arms and legs all gathered up with one of my hands while *my* arm and leg kept that tangle in place. Then, working as quickly as I could with my only free hand, I'd clean him before he could wiggle free and get to it.

Of course, there were days where I wasn't fast enough. *Ew.* I have to say, no amount of parenting experience will make me okay with that much poop smear. Which brings me to my point.

Even if it's mobile, a well set-up changing station is a necessity. Whether at home or away, do yourself a favor and grab what you'll need before you de-diaper.

- Steady surface. We used a dresser for the first few months.
- Changing pad. A proper one if you're on a high surface for safety, though never leave baby alone. For a bed, couch, or floor, just make sure it's something waterproof—surprise!
- Change of clothes for baby, just in case.
- Small basket of toys just for the changing station, to keep interest high.
- Unpackaged diapers. Trust me, out of the package is key!
- Wipes. Lots of them. And if I'm going in for poo, I pull them out of the package before I get started. No time to waste here, friends.
- Diaper cream for when needed.

Both my boys loved the changing table. By around six months, each would totally calm down when we laid them on it.

We'd just talk to them and they'd coo back. Those precious changing table chats are some of my favorite memories from their first years. Even with all the poop.

"As my boy grew, so did his poop. And as practiced as I was, I was totally unprepared for his newfound fascination with it."

Chapter 53

READ BOOKS.

On reading aloud to your baby.

Jelani Memory grew up in Portland, Oregon, and was raised by a single mother. A Black father of a blended family with six kids, there's rarely a dull moment in his home. He still lives in Portland and is the founder of A Kids Co. You can find him bouncing between five or so books, and he still reads to his kids every night before bed.

He/Him	6 Kids	Married	Black

TL;DR: It's important to read with your child, and to start early. Reading helps with language development, word acquisition, and bonding.

Amidst all of the ever-important activities that come with new parenthood, there is one activity that might initially get lost in the fray—reading! Start reading to your baby right away, even while they're still squarely in the belly.

You may feel like it's too early. I get it. I mean, they can't even understand what you're saying yet, right? Right. But the only way they can start to understand—not only what you're saying, but language itself—is if you share and expose them to it.

This awakening can be facilitated in a remarkable way by reading books to your kiddo. The cadence of your voice enunciating the words, expressing the vowels, and delivering a story gives your baby a remarkable gift—the more words that baby of yours hears, the better they develop language.

Reading.

The exchange goes beyond mere language acquisition. Believe it or not, your baby is bonding with you. Hearing your voice is one of the ways they connect with you, get to know you, and understand that they are safe. Think of reading as comforting white noise. Your voice becomes a part of the texture of sound your baby lives in.

If I may drop some science on you, even though babies are tiny, they already have LOTS of neurons in their brains. And guess what? Reading to them helps build neural pathways, which creates a foundation for learning. The more pathways, the more capable they'll have to learn as they grow up.[1]

I hope you're convinced that reading with your kid is important, but I'll give you one last reason why it's crucial. If you make time to read when they're little, they'll make time to read on their own later. It'll become a habit, and with all the changing, feeding, burping, and everything else, this habit is a key one to form.

As they grow up, you'll find that some of your most special moments with them happen when you sit down and read together. The moments when they're engaged with a new story. The moments when you see them begin to understand the words and make connections, and and the moments when you are the most present together.

FUN FACT: Your kid can tell when you like what you are reading and enjoy the act of reading. They can also tell when you want to be done. Let them feel your love of reading and that joy (and the words themselves) will grow with them, along with all the beautiful things reading brings: adventure, storytelling, facts, language acquisition, vocabulary, and a sense of purpose. The good stuff!

---

[1]Gavin McGuire, "Three Ways Early Reading Benefits Infants' Development," First Book, January 29, 2018, https://firstbook.org/blog/2018/01/29/three-ways-early-reading-benefits-infants-development/.

EVERYONE ELSE.

Tempting as it may be to keep baby all to yourself, you eventually have to share them with the world. With that comes a ton of feelings, questions, and fear. It's normal to hesitate as you navigate things like babysitters, in-laws, social media, and your changing social circle.

Introducing your baby, and your changing family, to the world can feel like a pretty big challenge, but it's necessary for a balanced and healthy life. This section of the book goes beyond diapers and burp cloths and explores the world on the other side of your comfort zone—and it's not as scary as you think. You'll hear from parents, caregivers, and experts who believe in the power of the village as well as the power of healthy boundaries.

Chapter 54

SOCIAL MEDIA.

Don't believe the hype—every parent struggles.

Conz Preti is a journalist with decades of experience in online media. She's from Argentina but currently lives in Maine with her husband, Zach, son, Ozzy, twin daughters, Luna and Ruby, and their rescue pup, Violet. Conz is raising her children bilingual, just like her parents raised her.

She/Her/Ella	3 Kids	Married	Latina

TL;DR: Comparing yourself to filtered and curated imagery is a losing battle. Instead, use social media to align with parents like yourself so you can feel validated, not intimidated.

Your baby is finally asleep and you have five minutes to browse social media and maybe share a photo of your little one with the world. You see post after post of brand-new moms (some still fresh from delivery) looking like they're ready for the Oscars.

You, on the other hand, are in sweats, covered in breast milk, and haven't showered in...when was the last time?

It's easy to feel discouraged by what we see online. We forget that behind those perfectly manicured feeds lies the same mess all new parents deal with—poopy explosions, sleepless nights, piles of neglected laundry. We will *never* know what's on the other side of the camera, or the amount of help celebrities and influencers have in their day-to-day lives.

Don't let social media bring you down. Instead, look for parents doing things that inspire you—whatever that may be.

For example, I started following parents of twins when I was pregnant with mine because I wanted to best prepare for what was coming. I also asked them tons of questions and everyone was extremely helpful, even with different parenting styles.

On the flip side, you can do more than simply consume social media. When I struggled with breastfeeding and felt completely alone because everyone on Facebook and Instagram seemed to have a fabulous breastfeeding journey, I posted about my experience. I thought, "If I'm going through this, someone else surely is too," and I was right.

The support I received from strangers who went through similar struggles was immense. In return, so many first-time parents thanked me for my honesty and transparency.

If you don't want to share anything on social media, don't feel pressured—there are no rules. Just because you didn't have an Instagram-perfect birth announcement that went viral, that is no reflection on who you will be as a parent. Only you can decide that.

"We will *never* know what's on the other side of the camera, or the amount of help celebrities and influencers have in their day-to-day lives."

Chapter 55

BOUNDARIES FOR FAMILY.

How to ask for help by making a family plan.

Myleik Teele is a multi-hyphenate career woman with many passions and interests, born and raised in Inglewood, California. She is a Black mom raising two tots, Noah (3) and Olivia (1), with her life partner, Daniel, who is white.

She/Her	2 Kids	Partnered	Black

TL;DR: After the arrival of a new baby, you may find that your family is eager to be tagged in to help. But even help can be overwhelming if you don't approach it mindfully. A family plan for engaging supportive relatives can preserve everyone's sanity.

Everyone seemed to be obsessed with the birth plan. Birth at home or in a hospital? Waterbirth? Natural birth or epidural?

No one told me to have a plan for the in-laws.

For the record, my children's grandparents are top-notch—the kind dreams are made of. However, looking back on my experience with them in the early days of parenthood, I realize that I should have taken a more organized approach when accepting their help.

How do you want to feel when you bring your baby home from the hospital? Write that down and share that with your partner. Everyone needs to be aligned with your expectations in those first few months after the baby gets home. If you don't want any advice, add that to the plan too.

Some other things to consider including in your postpartum family plan are:

Visitor logistics.

If they're not local, are they staying at your house or nearby? I vote for nearby so you get some time to yourself. Having guests in your home while you're constantly swapping out a jumbo pad from all the bleeding, waiting for the stool softener to kick in, and whipping out your boobs all day—every day—can be a lot. Consider giving your family a set of visiting hours, so they know when to drop by.

Assigning tasks.

Everyone visiting needs to know they're coming to work. Visitors should also prepare to help with little to no direction for things like meal prep, laundry clean up, and errands. In addition, you'll likely need help with all the things that need to be built for babies (like changing tables and bassinets), so be sure you know who is good with tools.

Presenting the plan.

Having a plan tends to land better than telling your family they can't see the new baby whenever they want. But, when it comes to in-laws, have your partner share the plan with them.

In other words, whoever knows the family visitors best should present the plan, so the stress of communicating doesn't fall on the birthing parent by default.

Being flexible.

Like a birth plan, if you get minutes or hours into your postpartum family plan and need to adjust it, then do that. You have the right to change your mind, even if you have careful blueprints. And let's be honest, how many "birth plans" go as planned?

Guarding your boundaries in those first few months is imperative as you establish a relationship with yourself as a parent.

Chapter 56

HOW TO INVOLVE FAMILY.

Nurturing your baby's family bonds.

Jennifer A. Perry has eight nieces and nephews who have taught her important lessons about kindness, resilience, curiosity, risk-taking, American history, basketball, French food, fairytale villains, and much more. She is involved in the lives of kids, too, as a creator of children's books and other educational content and as a literacy volunteer in her native New York City, which just happens to be one of the best places on the planet to have family adventures.

She/Her	8 Nieces & Nephews	Heterosexual	White

TL;DR: Cultivating meaningful relationships between your baby and extended family can lead to a wider circle of love, which lasts a lifetime. However, these connections can't happen on their own. Helping baby bond with extended family requires intention.

My twenty-something niece and I recently met for a long weekend in a city new to both of us. We hit "pause" on other important obligations and took separate planes, trains, and automobiles to meet there. But we made it happen, as we have many other times since our first journey together—when she was ten.

I am close to all my nieces and nephews for a simple reason that isn't simple at all: my sister, brother, and their spouses fostered my active involvement in their children's lives from the day they were each born. But, of course, that's easier said than done. Like every meaningful bond, these relationships take:

How To Involve Family.

Patience. Honesty.
Trial and error. Flexibility.
Perspective. Mutual respect.

Most of all, they require a commitment to embracing the power of moments. Long-lasting attachments don't just happen. You have to help make them happen. Try to go beyond group events and social media posts to create close personal connections between your child and your family (and friends you consider family).

Babies begin to develop essential bonds with adults during everyday moments. If you're lucky to have family nearby, invite their participation during mealtime, bath time, bedtime, playtime, and other daily routines—even if just to be present. Don't worry about your family's expectations. Most will love to hold baby while you're cooking, dry them off after a bath, take them for a walk around the neighborhood, or sit with them in the car while you pick up groceries.

If a family member wants a little one-on-one time with your child, encourage it! My mother makes up silly songs as she changes diapers. I am the "story time aunt" with lots of voices. My father whispers delightful secrets to sleepy babies in the moonlight. Your family's alone time with baby, no matter how brief, builds trust, comfort, memories, and, of course, love.

Although your child is the main focus, remember to give the bonus adults a moment of applause too. A quick "thank you" text or call goes a long way. I have large, padded envelopes overflowing with cards and letters from my siblings' kids long before they could write or even talk.

We all know that the more people who love and support your baby, the more secure and happy they'll be. So cultivate each of your baby's relationships as the unique gift it is—moment by moment by moment by moment.

"Babies begin to develop essential bonds with adults during everyday moments."

Chapter 57

LETTING FAMILY HELP.

Parenting is hard, and it's okay to ask for help.

Jucel Christine Erroba is a first-generation Filipina immigrant who is married to an artist extraordinaire with two "kids"—one daughter and one dog-hter (dog daughter). In her spare time, she likes to watch crime television shows and spend time with her village.

She/Her	2 Kids	Married	Asian/Pacific Islander

TL;DR: Being a working parent is hard for many reasons, but it's especially difficult to miss your kid while you're away for the day. Having family you trust nearby who are willing and able to care for your child can be a huge help in making that transition back to work.

I've heard the phrase "it takes a village to raise a child" a million times, but I didn't truly understand the meaning until I was at the end of my maternity leave and a blubbering mess on my first day back at work. I remember taking my first breast pump break and realizing the pump my workplace provided me was missing parts, so I couldn't pump. I was standing there, heavily engorged and sobbing because I just wanted to be home with my daughter, Ophelia. My village at that moment was my best friend, who drove to my house to pick up my breast pump and deliver it to me at my job across town. What a gem!

As I continued to ease back into working full-time, I began to realize just how much I was missing in my daughter's life. The creeping irrational thought of, "What if she forgets about me?" was always present, and there were many moments of staring blankly at the computer screen with tears silently rolling down my face.

Letting Family Help.

It was hard, and sometimes, it felt nearly impossible.

I would often question my purpose at work when I had this little baby at home who needed me. In reality though, my daughter couldn't have been in better hands. She had support every day from her father (my husband), maternal and paternal grandparents. Not to mention a sprinkling of aunts and uncles. While daycare is great, I felt my daughter being with her family was truly the best-case scenario for me.

By involving my family and pursuing my career, I taught my daughter important family and feminist values, so she would know that every person is equal no matter what their gender is. Or in other words: the skills she will need for building independence and the foundation for her future working self. One day, if she wants to, she can also go to work *and* care for her own child.

I was trusting our village to take care of and teach her how to be an amazing human being.

Now that my daughter is a bit older, we have started the conversation around preschool and kindergarten. We ultimately decided to hold off on sending Ophelia to school until she was in kindergarten because we believe she is already getting her preschool-level education from her village—her grandparents, on both sides, have taught her music, letters, and numbers. But more than that, they've taught her the invaluable lesson of how to be unique, kind, and smart.

I like to think my daughter is as brilliant as she is because of the positive influences she has around her. I couldn't have asked for a better outcome because I trust my child is safe and loved by those watching her, and that, in turn, makes it easier for me to do my job. And after a long day of work, nothing is better than hugs and kisses from my daughter.

"I was trusting our village to take care of and teach her how to be an amazing human being."

Chapter 58

FINDING COMMUNITY.

When you need it most is sometimes the hardest time to ask for help.

Karney Dunah is a servant of God and married to Lydia with four children, now adults. Raised as a pastor's kid in Liberia, West Africa, where he went into full-time ministry at age twenty-two, he now lives in Montgomery, Illinois, serving as executive director for the nonprofit organization United Liberia Inland Church Associates & Friends (ULICAF), which has ministry outreach in Liberia.

4 Kids	Married

TL;DR: Build a community of people you trust who have knowledge and experience in parenthood. Be humble and reach out to them in times of need. That may be the best parenting decision you ever make.

My name is Karney Dunah. I was born, raised, and married in Liberia and migrated to the US at the age of thirty-two. I am a father of four children, two boys and two girls. The first two, a boy and a girl, were born in Liberia. The last two, a girl and a boy, were born in the US. They're all adults now.

A baby is a blessing from God. A life you have been trusted with to care for up through adulthood. Parenthood can be very challenging and a sometimes lonely place to be, so you should not and cannot do it alone. The African proverb that says, "It takes a village to raise a child," should be embraced by all parents—especially those just starting out.

To be a good parent, build a trusted community you can reach out to in times of need. This may include your own parents, family members, friends, and community members who have been where you are today. They have knowledge and experience with both success and failure in parenthood, which you can learn from. The key to building this community, and a village lifestyle, is trust.

Our older son and daughter were born during a very brutal civil war in Liberia. We lived in the rebel-held area, and you could not find sanitary cloth diapers to purchase for babies. Concerned for the health of our daughter, we reached out to my uncle, a businessman, and asked him to purchase some for us from a marketplace shared by the warring parties. My uncle's assistance helped us care for our daughter during a desperate time.

In 1998, when we were expecting our first American-born baby, a family from our church reached out and told us to call them when it came time to have the baby. It was around four o'clock in the morning when I had to make that call. They came to our apartment, took our two older kids, and cared for them until we returned home from the hospital with our new baby. For the next twelve months, that family brought a box of the right-sized diapers for the baby to church almost every Sunday. A true godsend.

As you walk out of the hospital with that newborn baby, remember that there will be situations and circumstances you cannot handle. There will be places you cannot go and things that are totally impossible for you to do alone. In those times, have the courage to reach out to a trusted family member or member of your community and ask for help. This may be the best parenting decision you ever make.

If you have a need, question, or concern about your newborn, do your homework, but don't do it alone—turn to your community. You should be humble as new parents and quick to accept kindness from members of your trusted community. You should listen to words of wisdom and advice from them as well. I know that helped me and my family.

Name:	Phone Number/Email:

"...have the courage to reach out to those you trust and ask for help. This may be the best parenting decision you ever make."

| **Chapter 59**

COMBATTING COMPARISON.

How not to despair in the quest to compare.

Sylvia Farbstein is the proud mom of 24-year-old Brooke and 21-year-old Brandon. She has the privilege of working alongside Brandon, whose professional speaking career she helped launch when he was seventeen years old. Sylvia and her husband, Steve, live in Richmond, Virginia, and together they have learned that parenting is not a one-size-fits-all journey, and growth is experienced from the inside out.

She/Her	2 Kids	Married

TL;DR: With the onslaught of parenting advice and constant display of "perfection" on social media, it can be all too easy to compare your child to those around them. Remember that you have the gift of raising someone completely unique and special, and honoring what makes them who they are is one of the best things you can do as a parent.

You bring your precious newborn home from the hospital and are in awe of this marvelous human who seems to be perfect in every way. As the days and months set in, family and friends visit and they can't help but share advice about how to take care of your baby based on their experience with their children.

While it is lovely to find comfort in shared experiences, too much advice can cause you to start questioning whether you are doing things right. You may worry whether you will live up to the responsibility of raising your child as *they* say you should.

Combatting Comparison.

You take your infant to the pediatrician's office for well-baby checkups, and before you know it, your child is tracked on a percentile growth chart. While my daughter, Brooke, met the typical milestones and progressed as expected on the chart, my son, Brandon, did not. His skeletal condition (a rare form of dwarfism called metatropic dysplasia) significantly impacted his growth.

Brandon's development was on his own timeline.

My son's condition taught me early on not to despair in the quest to compare. The truth is, *every* child is on their own timeline. When we see them for who they are rather than constantly compare their progress to others—including their own siblings—we honor their uniqueness. Rather than raise our children in a sea of sameness, we should recognize and celebrate their individual needs and talents.

There is no blueprint, playbook, or linear path.

As you engage with your baby, give yourself grace and know that you are doing the best you can to provide them with a loving, safe environment. Don't compare the highlight reels on social media to the behind-the-scenes mess you experience. Savor the joy in the parenthood journey (especially the challenging parts), for you have the privilege to raise a soul who is unlike any other person out there. And that is an incomparable adventure that will push you to grow in unimaginable ways—no matter where your child falls on the growth chart.

"The truth is, *every* child is on their own timeline. When we see them for who they are rather than constantly compare them to others—including their own siblings—we honor their uniqueness."

Take it one day at a time.

Chapter 60

NEW SOCIAL REALITY.

Making friends with other parents isn't always easy to do.

Lauren Winfrey is a broadcast journalist who stepped away from the newsroom to work as a stay-at-home mom (SAHM) and care for her son. In her spare time, she loves exploring her new city of Philadelphia with her husband, Mike, her son, MJ, and her maltipoo, Bo.

She/Her	2 Kids	Married	Black

TL;DR: A lot of things change when you become a new parent, including your friendships. And it's hard when no one can relate to you. Building new relationships with other parents takes time and in the meantime, it gets lonely. Until new friendships blossom, give yourself grace, and stay present with your special little one.

As a new parent, you might not recognize your reflection when you look in the mirror.

Your body is different. Those bags under your eyes must have been delivered to the wrong address because you don't remember adding them to the cart. Just as you begin to sit for a few minutes of rest, baby cries—and you cry a little too. Baby's ready for a diaper change and more milk. You're ready to crawl under the covers. This is the exhausting journey that is motherhood, and it's just the beginning.

Things change when you become a parent, and we don't often talk about to what extent. Likely because it's different for each of us.

I struggled to make friends as a new mom. Eighteen months into motherhood and thanks to a move to the East Coast, I'm still struggling. I have one friend who's a mom—we've been friends since high school—and the rest of my friends are single. And try as they might, it's a struggle to feel like we can relate to one another the way we used to. This doesn't mean I love my friends less; it simply means there's a longing to connect with those sharing my experience. Because without that connectedness, loneliness creeps in.

And in those moments of loneliness, when thoughts that no one "gets it" begin to settle into your soul, allow yourself to feel, but try not to wallow. Befriending other parents will come, but in the meantime, ask for the support of your non-parent friends—fostering those relationships is equally as important.

Allow yourself grace when you can't make it to every social event, or because your travel calendar isn't as robust as it once was. It's okay. If your goal is to get back to catching flights, you will.

Your current season isn't your forever season. And when that little human you created looks up at you cooing and smiling with those big, beautiful eyes, every sacrifice will be worth it.

The price of raising a happy, whole human while remaining a happy, whole human cannot be quantified. But it's worth it.

"Befriending other parents will come, but in the meantime, soak up the support of your non-parent friends—fostering those relationships is equally as important."

Chapter 61

POSSESSIVENESS.

Is it love or obsession?

Megan Laney was born and raised in Oregon's Willamette Valley, where—being a middle child—she developed an active imagination and a knack for getting out of trouble when she caused mischief. She works in marketing and communications in Portland, Oregon, and is raising two boys with her husband. RIP "having nice things."

She/Her	2 Kids	Married	Mexican American

TL;DR: That new little person you just brought home is about to be pretty popular. Sometimes, handing them over to friends and family is an anxiety-inducing milestone. Take a breath, accept your new bear-like parental instincts, and find a happy balance.

I think, rationally, we all know that we're going to love our kids. Before I had my first son, I didn't consider myself to be a "kid person," even though I had heard it would be different once I had my own. I accepted that, but I expected to be a chill mom. I would be objective about my own kid. Cool, not codependent.

So it came as a complete shock to me when I became instantly obsessed with my newborn. No, beyond obsessed. I was like Golem from *The Lord of the Rings*—wholly entranced by my baby and suspicious of everyone else's methods and motivations.

Suddenly, my mother and mother-in-law were just other women vying for my son's love. My husband was a supportive and attentive but ultimately ineffective caretaker. When going to family events, I would "forget" to bring extra bottles of milk so I could use breastfeeding as an excuse to snatch him away from Great Aunt *Name Here.*

Eventually, going back to work and having to hand him over to a team of wonderful, loving women at his daycare weaned me off my possessiveness a bit. I learned that I actually needed a real break to feel like myself—the person I'd spent over thirty years cultivating before he came along. I learned that it's perfectly okay to obsess over newborns. It's actually natural and totally normal. And it's okay to not want to pass your new tiny creation around from person to person.

These are the markings of a truly chill mom.

So, don't worry about snapping out of it. It's a special time and you should bond as much as you possibly can with your baby, in the way you prefer. While writing this, I gave birth to my second son, and it's been very different from my first experience. Now, I hold different things closely, like my relationship with my older son, as I help him to know and love his baby brother.

And I take time for showers. Really long showers.

"It's okay to not want to pass your new tiny creation around from person to person."

Chapter 62

LIVING FAR AWAY.

What happens when your village is in another time zone?

Tiffany Rose Smith is a storyteller, creative entrepreneur, mother of two, and partner to one. She is a proud, Black, biracial southerner who spent her adult years between New York City and Los Angeles but has since settled in Austin, Texas.

She/Her	2 Kids	Black Biracial

TL;DR: Having a baby with no friends or family around can feel incredibly isolating, but creating a village from scratch takes effort, so it can be tempting to try to go it alone. Know that the village you'll build is worth it.

We've all heard it takes a village to raise a child. So what happens when your most trusted bunch is across an ocean or on another coast? After spending the first five years of my parenting journey 3,000 miles away from my people, I learned some things.

Cultivate a community wherever you go.

If this lifelong introvert with social anxiety can do it, so can you. Take the classes, go to the park, be open to befriending other parents wherever you go. Once, I met a new mom-friend at an open house—without even trying!

Leave room for others to love on you and your family, and one day you'll look through those tired eyes and find yourself surrounded by a tribe.

A virtual village is still a village.

Between visits, family video chats and virtual watch parties with your favorite friends can do wonders. The ongoing group chats with faraway cousins to compare unusual baby behaviors—all of these things matter.

Just because you're building new relationships doesn't mean your existing relationships can't offer support in unique ways.

Tap into whatever resources are available.
Parenting is a big job, especially when rolling solo, so source all the help available and use it. This could mean taking advantage of the perks from your healthcare provider, budgeting for a post-partum doula, or accepting that meal your neighbor offered. We never turn down prepared food.

Say yes when your favorite child-free coworker offers to come by while you nap. Maybe leave a basket of unfolded laundry lying around and see what happens.

Make peace with your unique situation.
Try not to waste time comparing your circumstances to that friend with superhero grandparents next door. On the other side of gritted-teeth acceptance that I am far from family, I found a pleasant surprise. In the absence of consistent input, I relied heavily on my own intuition. So, now, I'm braver, more ground-ed, and my family is the kind of close that dreams are made of.

I hope this helps. But if you find yourself feeling like an exhaust-ed, stain-ridden island, come back here, read this, and remem-ber home is where you make it.

"Leave room for others to love on you and your family, and one day you'll look through those tired eyes and find yourself surrounded by a tribe."

Chapter 63

ANTI-SHAME PARENTING PILLARS.

Never be ashamed of what you or your child need.

Dominique Matti is a mother of two, a medicine maker, and a diviner. She lives and works in Philadelphia where she writes primarily about healing.

She/Her	Single	Queer	Black

TL;DR: With new parenthood comes a wave of expectations, advice, and yes, shame. But babies don't come with an instruction manual for a reason—the process requires you figure most of it out as you go.

I became pregnant with my first child when I was twenty-one. I was a house cleaner by day and a musician by night and adjusting to a new city and a new marriage. My baby was unplanned, but I welcomed him with joy (and a healthy dose of trepidation). So I started looking for input and advice from parenting forums.

Parenting forums, like any space that provides advice, can be a source of shame and confusion. The suggestions and tips often exist in stark contrast with one another and can feel fatalistic. On the one hand, you will traumatize your baby if you let them cry. But, on the other hand, your baby will never self-soothe if you don't let them cry.

Eventually, I learned how to seek advice and information without feeling pressured or shamed.

Here are my anti-shame parenting pillars:

Give yourself some grace.
Surround yourself with those who have plenty of grace for you as well, because you're doing a brand-new thing. Though you may feel a prevailing sense that the stakes are unbearably high (love will do that), know that a bit of clumsiness is inevitable.

Try and fail.
You can decide to stay home and then decide to go back to work. You can decide to breastfeed and then switch to formula. You can attempt to co-sleep and then choose to sleep train. Adaptability is a skill worth cultivating in any relationship. Ultimately, you are developing a relationship with that small person looking up at you.

Know your limits.
There is no shortage of the notion that all parents should be bottomless, sleepless wells. But that doesn't have to be you. Knowing your limits requires you to build a relationship with yourself and learn who you are in this new context.

Whether you feel shame from a thousand battling voices online or within your community of friends and family, release it. This process is meant to be a learning experience, and the information that resonates with you will inform how parenting looks for you and your child—two people no one knows better than you.

"There is no shortage of the notion that parents should be bottomless, sleepless wells."

Chapter 64

FINDING CARE.

Finding the right fit for your family is a process.

Charnaie Gordon is a diversity and inclusion expert, author, podcast host, and digital creator. She also serves on the National Advisory Board for Reading is Fundamental for their Race, Equity, and Inclusion (REI) initiative.

She/Her	2 Kids	Married	Black

TL;DR: Making the decision to find outside care for your child can be overwhelming, but know that what matters is what works best for your family. Have confidence in the choice you make to bring in extra care and support.

As a new parent, I approached the thought of leaving my babies with someone else for the first time with a lot of mixed emotions. And tears.

I didn't want to leave my kids with just anyone. It was hard to choose a location outside the comforting familiarity of our home and entrust my kids' care to a new person. Since my husband and I worked full-time, we chose to send our kids to daycare.

It took us a while to find the right fit for our family—one that made us all feel comfortable, safe, and loved. If you're in the phase of finding care for your little ones, you may have some anxiety circulating within you like I did. And that is okay.

Although finding care was not an easy task, I did learn a few ways to cope during that challenging season.

Make a plan.

Set a budget, do your own research, and ask lots of questions when choosing a provider.

Own your decision to find outside care.

Don't be deterred if your first choice isn't the best experience—mine wasn't. Ultimately, I had to learn to trust my gut and the decision that outside care was best for our family, even when it took multiple tries to get it right.

Embrace the roller coaster of emotions.

Giving myself permission to bawl my eyes out was important for me. I was an emotional mess and was much less productive at work until I finally found my rhythm. It was a process (and I recommend you keep plenty of tissues on hand for the transition period).

Cherish the time with your little ones.

It was important for me not to completely replace my presence with childcare. Children still need to feel that connection to their parents or primary caregivers. For me, that meant spending two hours of quality time with them before winding down with our bedtime routine.

Finding care can be tough, so take plenty of deep breaths. Remember that many parents have been through this milestone before you. And many will come after you.

Somebody hand me a tissue!

"Ultimately, I had to learn to trust my gut that outside care was best for our family, even though it took multiple tries to get it right."

Chapter 65

SIBLINGS.

Helping your older child adjust to a newborn.

Kherri Jean lives in the Dallas/Fort Worth area. She is married and a mother to two sons, ten and five years old. She loves to travel, read, and eat molten lava chocolate cake.

She/Her	2 Kids	Married	African American

TL;DR: Welcoming a baby to the family inevitably alters the dynamic and sometimes, newly older siblings struggle with sharing that attention previously reserved just for them. Help your children understand that each one of them will need undivided attention from you at different times. So, set aside intentional, one-on-one time with each kid.

I always wanted two children, but after enduring a very difficult labor, delivery, and postpartum experience with my first son, I wasn't so sure about reliving that experience so quickly.

As a result, we waited...one year, two years, three years, four years. Finally, five years later, we decided it was time to try again. Thankfully, my next delivery and postpartum process was much smoother, and I was happy I embarked upon the motherhood journey again.

Everything was great until we brought our youngest son home from the hospital. His big brother was initially excited, but that blissful feeling evaporated quickly. As time that was normally reserved for our oldest son began to diminish, I noticed a marked change in the way he interacted with us.

Siblings.

For example, I remember an incident during our newborn photography shoot. My husband and I were focused on capturing as many "picture-perfect" poses with our napping baby as we could, when our oldest son interrupted the shoot to tell us (and show us) the "new book" he had just written.

It was time to sit down and talk. I told him that I knew this adjustment might be difficult but that there would be times when baby brother would need our undivided attention (like when he needed to be nursed or changed) and times when, he too, would need that same kind of attention. I reassured him I was very interested in seeing his book, but *it would have to wait* for a time when we could fully focus on him.

Over the past five years, we have had other instances where the boys compete for attention, but they are few and far between. The balance between sharing time and making each child a priority can be difficult to manage, but my husband and I try to divide and conquer where it makes sense.

We also realize the importance of being intentional about spending one-on-one time with each of them and doing their favorite things, like watching the same movie for the millionth time with my youngest son or going head-to-head in a video game with my oldest.

There is no perfect science to sharing love and attention evenly. Sometimes one kid will feel slighted, but it is critical to remind them of how important they are to you, one hug, kiss, and "I love you" at a time.

"The balance between sharing time and making each child a priority can be difficult to manage, but my husband and I try to divide and conquer where it makes sense."

Chapter 66

BABYSITTERS.

There's an upside to inviting strangers over.

Yasmin Fathi is a married mother of a two-year-old girl. She moved to the US from Iran in 2010, works as an architect, and runs a home inspection and real estate business. Yasmin loves art—especially music—and learning about different cultures in the world.

1 Kid	Heterosexual	Persian Iranian

TL;DR: Choosing a babysitter for your baby is an important decision which requires a lot of trust and confidence. But inviting trusted new caregivers into your baby's life is a gift—both for your child and for you.

My whole life, I have defined myself as an independent working professional. In my last days of maternity leave, hugging my four-month-old, I started thinking about how useful I once was and how much I missed working and using my brain!

Then, suddenly, the fear of leaving my needy baby alone made me burst into tears. I held her close and asked her to be strong because I needed to go back to work to be a healthy and happy mom for her.

I made my decision. So I called a babysitter I knew through a friend. I gave her some guidelines the first few days about how frequently to change my baby's diaper, when to put her down for a nap, and how to prepare her snacks and meals.

Finding Care.

On my first day back to work, my baby sensed I was going away and cried hard. I left home quickly and cried in my car, telling myself I was doing the right thing.

As I drove to work, I listened to my favorite music and talked to my best friend, and was so joy-filled to have the time to do that. I kept an eye on the new babysitter through our security camera, and although she was caring and kind, she wasn't as perfect as I wanted her to be.

"Why is she putting diapers on my baby like this? Why isn't she doing it the exact way I do it? Am I being too controlling? Am I being too sensitive?"

I kept reminding myself it's okay to compromise some of the rules I made for myself with my baby. Her babysitter, an older woman, was like a kind grandmother to my daughter, which was perfect for our family. I knew she was safe and happy.

When coming back to my baby at the end of the day, I was surprised to find my love for her had deepened. I was full of energy and overall a happier mom, playing with her patiently for hours.

Now I'm so glad I stood up for myself. I needed to work to be able to feel confident again.

Getting help from a babysitter while I worked out of the house made me a better and happier mom.

My baby knows in her heart that, no matter what, her loving mom will always come back to her.

"When coming back to my baby at the end of the day, I was surprised to find my love for her had deepened."

Chapter 67

PHYSICAL BOUNDARIES.

Teaching babies the power of "no" before they learn to say it.

Qimmah Saafir is a single, working mother of a five-year-old. She has a loving co-parent, a supportive partner, and a huge family...and still has to feel her way through this thing. It's just Qimmah and Lehan at home, and they take things day by day. And that is more than okay. For her and for you.

She/Her	Woman	Black

TL;DR: New babies have the habit of attracting a lot of curious people. They want to touch and hold and share space with the newest human in the room. Exercising your right to space as a parent comes with a bonus—you're also teaching your baby how to create boundaries.

My daughter, Leahn, has always been a light. And by light, I mean a little being who draws people to her, always. I remember walking with her in the stroller through the city. Literal crowds of people would form, all coming to look at her.

As a new mother, it was terrifying. But I absolutely understood it. She is physically beautiful but also has an undeniable energy. A pull, if you will. I have had to adjust to this reality.

Will I ever be fully okay with how strangers respond and want to interact with my daughter? More than likely, no. But I try.

Physical Boundaries.

My discomfort stems from the innate protectiveness of any mother as well as my own trauma-related reactions that arise. I had to learn to do away with the shame of that. I also had to learn to trust myself as her mother and create the parameters I see fit for my child.

Here's the thing: That is YOUR baby. Please never let anyone guilt or shame you into ignoring your intuition when it comes to keeping your baby safe.

I also can't stress enough the importance of teaching your baby the usage of boundaries and the word "no"—even before they know how to say it. For example, I would gently move Lehan out of their reach if someone approached her. (Yes, people can be rude and ignore you, the parent, while approaching your child.) This made them aware of their actions and sometimes prompted them to ask me if it was okay to engage with her.

Just because you have a baby and that baby is adorable does not grant open access to anyone who wishes to interact. You get to decide. You get to be selective. You get to be protective. You get to have boundaries.

The sooner you allow your child to witness you exercising those boundaries, the sooner they begin to learn that they can also.

"Please never let anyone guilt or shame you into ignoring your intuition when it comes to keeping your baby safe."

SECTION FOUR

YOU, TOO.

Believe it or not, the first year of parenthood has more to do with you than your baby. Yes, your baby will be the focus of most conversations for the foreseeable future. You'll make lots of choices that center on your baby's well-being. But, a critical asset for a successful first year of parenthood is you. Yes, you.

Among the hundreds of exciting milestones will be sleepless nights, arguments with your partner, changes to your social circle, and a slew of other things you maybe never considered before becoming a parent. As you're on this journey, it's important to remember you must stay healthy and well so you can show up in the best way for your family. This section of the book is all about you—the parent—the person who that beautiful new human depends on.

Chapter 68

NAVIGATING YOUR FEELINGS.

Parenting is hard and amazing—it's totally normal to have all the feels.

Dr. Becky Kennedy is a clinical psychologist who specializes in parenting, anxiety, and resilience; she's also a mom of three. She loves to translate deep ideas about parenting and mental health into practical, actionable strategies. But please know this too: even with all her training, Dr. Becky is the first to say parenting is really hard for her, full of challenging moments, frustrations, and difficult feelings—she's in the trenches with all of you.

| She/Her | 3 Kids | Married | Heterosexual |

TL;DR: Parents, acknowledge your feelings, validate them, and permit yourself to feel how you feel to fully apply yourself to the heart of the job: being present for yourself and your baby.

It's okay to have lots of feelings about being a parent. In fact, it's normal! I'm not just talking about these feelings: excited, in love, fulfilled. I'm also talking about these feelings: exhausted, frustrated, overwhelmed, sad, aggravated.

Having a kid is amazing and having a kid is also challenging. You will have moments when you feel grateful and content and others when you feel resentful and out of control—and you will likely have moments when you feel all these feelings at once. Knowing we can have a lot of feelings at the same time is key to maintaining our mental health. After all, it's rarely our feelings themselves that make us feel awful—it's our reactions to our feelings that send us into despair. Let's look at an example.

It's Saturday morning. You're exhausted and wish you could stay in bed, but you hear your baby crying. You know that cry means, "I'm hungry!" You find yourself thinking, "I want to be doing anything but feeding my baby right now!" You're frustrated, sad, and overwhelmed.

Now what? Well, how we feel comes from how we react to this set of thoughts and emotions.

Option 1

We worry and judge ourselves: "I'm not supposed to feel this way! What awful thoughts. I should feel lucky I have a baby!" What happens next? We experience shame and guilt, which makes our initial feelings bigger and heavier. We then feel worse and things start to feel impossible. We tell ourselves we are bad parents.

Option 2

We acknowledge, validate, and permit our emotions and thoughts (I call this "AVP"). We tell ourselves, "I'm noticing lots of the hard feelings parenthood brings. It makes sense I'm feeling this way—after all, parenting and getting out of bed when you're tired is tough! I'm giving myself permission to feel frustrated and sad and overwhelmed. All feelings are in motion and generally pass." What happens next? Our feelings feel *seen*. They remain but become less intense. Life feels more manageable.

Let's tie this all together with three takeaways:
1. Good parents have a range of feelings about parenthood.
2. There are moments you'll feel excited, happy, content, angry, sad, and confused.
3. Acknowledge all your feelings, including the tough ones! Validate them. Permit them to be there.

You've got this.

Chapter 69

THE JUGGLE.

The juggle is real. And the responsibilities don't have to be all on you.

Joy Cho is a designer, creative director, wife, daughter, friend, boss, and mother of two (among lots of other things). She lives in Los Angeles with her family, doing her best to juggle what life throws her way.

She/Her	2 Kids	Thai American

TL;DR: Finding balance at home with your parenting partner means letting go of control and allowing them to pick up what you can't carry alone.

Here we are, managing our lives just fine and then along comes a baby—the perfect thing to throw everything off balance!

Before I had kids, I always figured out how to get things done. I created a goal, identified the steps to achieve the goal, did the steps, and checked the goal off my list. Whether big or small, it was relatively manageable. So I thought a baby would be another thing to manage.

Nope!

After my first baby (and then again after my second), I found myself overwhelmed and crying constantly. For the first six months, I didn't know how to handle all my responsibilities and also care for this new being. Then, one day, my husband came home to find me overcome with anxiety. I told him how overwhelmed I was. He asked why I didn't tell him I was feeling that way, and we discussed ways to relieve the stress.

That's when I realized I had made a lot of assumptions about how to be a good mother, partner, friend, and boss. I was putting all the responsibility on myself.

"I can do those things, too. I am in this with you," my husband said. That's when I realized I was holding the weight of it all on my shoulders when I didn't have to.

Things got a lot better once I expressed what I needed to others and allowed them to help. Of course, it's never easy to juggle it all, but it can be more manageable when you figure out what you can handle. Can your partner or family help with making meals or fixing things around the house? Can someone take your other children while you're with the baby? How can you outsource help like outside childcare or asking for support at work?

Remember, life will always change and seasons ebb and flow. Likewise, your parenting roles and responsibilities can change as your outside responsibilities (like your job) fluctuate. Maybe right now, you do dinner while your partner does bath time. You do drop-off and your partner does pick-up. But next month or next year, things may look different and you can divide and conquer differently as it makes sense for your family.

After all, it's not about achieving a perfect balance. It's about learning how to juggle the things you need to do and knowing it's okay to ask for help with it all.

"Of course, it's never easy to juggle it all, but it can be more manageable when you figure out what you can handle."

Chapter 70

STAYING CONNECTED.

Maintaining a special bond with your baby.

Rozonda "Chilli" Thomas is an American singer, dancer, actress, television personality, and model who rose to fame in the early 1990s as a member of group TLC on record, the best-selling girl group in the US. Chilli is passionate about her work as an advocate for children and her commitment to helping others develop a healthy lifestyle. Chilli credits her faith and commitment to her craft for the group's longevity and enjoys touring and performing across the country.

TL;DR: Leaning into the special bond you share with your baby can be a guiding light in times of uncertainty. Stay in tune with your baby and with yourself to keep that bond strong.

I always knew I wanted to be a mother, but after learning that I was pregnant with my son, Tron, I remember feeling a mix of extreme happiness and anxiety. Once you get that confirmation from the doctor it feels like your life changes immediately. I was nauseous all day for three months straight and had morning sickness until I gave birth. Eventually, I learned how to manage. And like most mothers, once my son was born, my biggest priority was being as healthy as I could be so he could have the best possible start.

Every mother's greatest wish is to have a healthy baby. It doesn't matter how old you are, where you're from, or whether you are single or married; mothers are focused on the well-being of that precious little baby. Through that work, we learn that our minds and bodies were made to do this job. My godmother once told me to lay my newborn baby to sleep on my chest because my heartbeat and breathing pattern would calm him and remind him to breathe. I believe it's important to maintain that divine connection with your baby, especially in the early months.

Here is my advice for staying in tune with your baby and with yourself:

Listen to that God-given voice.
When things get overwhelming, follow your instincts—that God-given voice. For example, if you feel you need to take your baby to the doctor, take them to the doctor. It doesn't matter if it turns out to be unnecessary—it's always better to err on the side of caution.

Take care of yourself.
It's easy to get wrapped up in the baby and not take time for yourself. So, when your baby sleeps, you need to sleep. Take every opportunity to get as much rest as possible, even if that means neglecting all the busy work you reserve for naptime— you'll need it.

Accept help when it's offered.
Don't turn down a helping hand because you think you have to do everything alone. It's a blessing to have people around who want to help. Let them.

Advice will come and go, but know you have everything you need inside of you to be the best parent God created you to be.

"My godmother told me to lay my newborn baby to sleep on my chest because my heartbeat and breathing pattern would calm him and remind him to breathe."

Chapter 71

PARENTING OURSELVES.

Broken records and creating our own playlist.

Kileah McIlvain is mom to four hobbits (two who are neurodiverse), a backyard chicken wrangler, chronically depressed, and the author of *A Kids Book About Depression*. She is a native of the Pacific Northwest and feels most at home in the verdant woods and coastal wilds of Washington state. You will most often find her knitting, gardening, reading voraciously, or talking to her hens instead of folding the laundry.

She/Her	4 Kids	Married	Heterosexual

TL;DR: Contrary to common belief, it is you who must grow in order to raise healthy kids.

We've been parents for thirteen years and we still feel new at this. But time has brought insight, and the key takeaway for us so far is not "do better" but rather "choose to unlearn what doesn't work, and work to learn what does."

Oh, we had ideals. We had our philosophies and plans about how we would do everything right. We created the "perfect playlist" for success, carefully prepared, packaged and placed on the pedestal of our eighteen-year parenting vision...and then *bam*. The fresh new arrival of eight pounds, six ounces began to slowly reveal our inexperience and gently unraveled our carefully-woven plans. More fresh humans were added to our numbers over the following years.

Reality revealed itself when sleep deprivation came along. "No" became the tiny-voiced proclamation of the hour, mental health issues surfaced, and life became a story of survival and doing whatever we could to cope.

Our inner voice, our "parent" voice, our childhood, played like a broken record. It was paralyzing, and we had to encounter our own parental reckoning. We discovered that parenting is as much about parenting ourselves and unlearning our past as it is about guiding and loving our kids.

That "perfect playlist" can't really accomplish much unless we adapt it to our family's needs. That broken record, that unraveling, is what taught us that we could do things differently.

These kids of ours have the unique ability to help us undo ourselves so that we can be remade into the best parents for our family. Our kids need to feel our love and see our own growth alongside theirs. A life that is failing, growing, changing, and healing speaks volumes more than methods and ideals.

We have been given the gift of parenting in our own way. To create our own playlist. It's okay to be new at this. We're new at this, too. Welcome.

"Our kids need to feel our love and see our own growth alongside theirs."

Chapter 72

SINGLE PARENTS RETURNING TO WORK.

You are not a statistic, you are a family.

Ashley Simpo is a single mother of a son named Orion. She is a writer, author, and editor living in Brooklyn, New York, by way of Oakland, California. Ashley is the author of *A Kids Book About Divorce* and has navigated the complex waters of single parenthood by leaning into her community and uplifting other parents through words of encouragement and support on her social media channels. Ashley and Orion love to tell jokes at dinner time, ride scooters through their neighborhood, and hang out with their pet guinea pig, Ginger.

She/Her	1 Kid	Divorced and Partnered	Black

TL;DR: Your leave is all used up and it's time to head back to work. How on earth do people even do this? Single parents are strong, capable, and they raise incredible, happy kids. Welcome to your new community; you're going to be just fine.

Before I was a mom, I was someone who didn't plan their life around having any kids. I told myself if I couldn't do it "right," I wouldn't do it at all. I wanted to find the perfect spouse, the perfect home, and have a beautifully perfect child whom I would nurture and care for full time until they were old enough for pre-school. Well, one of those things happened—I had a beautifully perfect child. The rest didn't turn out how I thought it would.

So, with a pending divorce and a brand-new parenting reality, I found myself returning to work way before I planned to. It was a tough pill to swallow, especially as someone raised by a stay-at-home mother. I had no idea what it would feel like to hand my little one over to a stranger and focus on work all day. But going back to work was important. As a single parent, I needed to build a stable career and create a consistent and safe environment for my son. I needed to find a way to feel complete at work and at home, even without the benefit of a helpful domestic partner. Since then I found ways to create balance in our lives and still pursue my career. Here's what I've learned.

Know your rights at work.
Parents and caregivers may experience discrimination in the workplace when it comes to things like taking time off to care for a sick child or having to opt out of after-work activities. Workplace discrimination impacts single parents. Research the laws in your state so you're aware of your rights.

Create your dream team.
Tap into the community you have and see who can be available to help out. Not just for the little things, like occupying the baby while you clean on weekends. But for the big things, like pick-up and drop-off or helping with sick care. If you have the means to do so, a helper or nanny can be an incredible asset.

Simplify any and everything.
Now is not the time to dwell on the details. Your most vital assets as a single working parent are your sanity and wellness. So learn to love a good hack. Cook for a day and stock your fridge and freezer with premade meals. Set up subscriptions for items you use a lot (toilet paper, batteries, water filters) so you never have to think twice or run out. Embrace the path of least resistance.

Stillness and self-care are now necessities.
Working and caring for a baby as a single parent is practically an Olympic event. Now more than ever, your mental health matters. Read books that provide tools for managing anxiety or stress,

work with a therapist or life coach to help you sort through the ups and downs as they come, journal, meditate, or pray—whatever you can do to let off steam and consistently find your balance. Avoiding burnout should be your highest priority.

If there's anything you take away from this, I hope it's this: Forgive yourself. Let go of the guilt that will bubble up as you wave goodbye to your little one and head off to work. It's okay. You're doing exactly what your family needs, and that makes you an incredible parent. Your child will grow into the family and life they have, as long as you meet them with love and support.

"As a single parent,
I needed to
build a stable
career and
create a
consistent
and safe
environment
for my son."

Chapter 73

THE CHOICE TO HAVE (ONLY) ONE.

It's okay to just have one child.

Jose Corona is a proud father, husband, brother, and son born in Mexico, raised in Watsonville, California, who now resides in Oakland, California—his adopted home for the last eighteen years. Jose is a firm believer that talent lies everywhere and within everyone, but opportunity does not. He tirelessly works to create environments and cultures where everyone—adults and children—has the opportunity to thrive.

He/Him	1 Kid	Male	Latino

TL;DR: You may feel pressure to have a big family, but you don't have to! Invasive questions and the occasional passive-aggressive comment aside, your people will come around eventually, and you'll feel better knowing you did what was best for you and your family.

"How is your baby doing, Jose?"

"Mateo? He's as good as can be."

"Are you guys thinking of having more?"

"Nope. We're one and done."

"Hmmm..." is what followed my answer, combined with a blank stare that led to an immediate change of subject to something like the weather.

I am not sure about you, but this conversation happened dozens of times with my family during the first year of having our son, Mateo. My dad is one of nine children, and my mom is one of eleven. All my aunts and uncles have multiple children, as did all my brothers at the time of Mateo's birth. So, it was almost an expectation that I would follow suit.

Choosing to only have one child came with a lot of pressure, and even a sense of guilt, which my wife and I carried for a long time. But I am here to tell you it is okay to be intentional about having one child.

My wife, Mary, and I chose to have one child because, well, that's all we wanted. Period. The truth is, raising a child is hard. That first year of Mateo's life was beautiful in so many ways. But it was also hard on us emotionally, physically, and financially. It was hard on our relationship with one another because all our attention was focused on Mateo.

And, that's how we felt with only *one* child! With both my wife and I having demanding careers, we couldn't imagine raising any more children. Some family members said we were selfish for just having one kid. They had no idea how hurtful that was to hear.

But you know what? Our family, ultimately, accepted our decision, or at least stopped bringing it up! More importantly, Mary and I were united around our decision. We know our small family unit is as much of a family as any family with multiple children.

Whatever your reason is for having one child, it's your decision. You know yourself best and you know what fits your life better than anyone.

"Choosing to only have one child came with a lot of pressure, and even a sense of guilt."

Chapter 74

SELF-CARE.

It's more than just a bubble bath.

Dr. Ann-Louise Lockhart , PsyD, loves taking on lots of different roles, including that of a pediatric psychologist, parent coach, author, wife of twenty-three years, and mom of two (ages nine and eleven). She is from the island of St. Croix and currently lives with her family in San Antonio, Texas.

She/Her	2 Kids	Married	West Indian

TL;DR: Self-care goes way beyond maintaining your personal hygiene and soaking in a bathtub. It means engaging in activities you value, being around supportive people, and replacing self-doubt with self-empowering encouragement.

Self-care is not a luxury. As a new parent, it is a necessity. Although taking care of your hygiene and basic daily needs are important, self-care goes way beyond alone time in the bathtub. It involves engaging in activities you value and being around people who support you. It's about acknowledging and caring for your thoughts. Self-care is a conscious act done intentionally to promote all parts of you and your health.

I was married twelve years before I had my first child at thirty-seven years old. I was what they called "advanced maternal age." As a psychologist and coach, I helped many parents through this exact experience, but I had never done it myself. I was scared. Self-doubt started to creep in. I realized it's different when it's your own journey.

When you're exhausted and the baby is not sleeping or feeding the way you expected, maybe these thoughts will show up:

- Why is this so hard for me?
- Why is it so easy for everyone else?
- What's wrong with me?
- Am I a good parent?
- This is too much.

Some version of these thoughts pop up for every parent. You can be excited about this new baby and also feel regret, emotional overwhelm, discouragement, and guilt.

You are allowed to have all the thoughts and feelings, even if they appear to conflict with one another. Mine certainly did.

Self-care is saying:

- This is hard because being a new parent is hard.
- It's not easy for everyone else.
- There is nothing wrong with me.
- I am a good parent.
- This baby is not too much for me.
- I will intentionally make time for things that are important to me.
- I will ask for real help and share the load.

It is likely your thoughts have become so automatic you don't even realize you are having them. When you address and take care of your thoughts, your body and mental well-being will follow.

That is true self-care.

"Self-care is a conscious act you do intentionally to promote all parts of you and your health."

Chapter 75

ARGUMENTS.

Engaging in conflict with wisdom and empathy.

Jonathan Simcoe and his wife are the proud parents of five beautiful children living near Portland, Oregon. Through faith, the ache of loss, and the beauty of shared creativity, they are shaping their children to be emotionally connected, courageously curious, and advocates for justice. You can find them playing outside, exploring their backyard garden, or creating their wildest dreams from their living room.

5 Kids	Married	White

TL;DR: Arguments will happen, and they'll even happen in front of your baby. But lovingly working through them will help your child learn that conflict is an opportunity, not a failure.

To quote R.E.M., "Everybody hurts sometimes."

Sometimes, when we are hurt, we reciprocate hurt to others. When our values and emotions conflict with other people, there can be friction and discord. This is true for adults, and it is certainly true for our children.

But despite what you might think or how you were raised, conflict is a really good thing. Conflict exists when different ways of seeing and feeling the world collide. It means we care. It means the person we are fighting with cares. But we need tools to ensure we navigate conflict and help our children begin to process conflict effectively.

Modeling something better.

As parents, our instincts are to protect our children from things in the grown-up world. There is wisdom in when and how we introduce our kids to hard things, but more than anything, our kids need good behavior modeled to them. Conflict is one area where parents can work together to model healthy interaction. The fact is, you are going to fight in front of your kids. You are going to have conflict with friends, family, and others. When you do, make sure you do not tear each other down. Babies learn from both the verbal and non-verbal cues, postures, and tones used to work through conflict.

Take time to cool off if you need it. If a conflict starts while your children are watching, resolve the conflict in front of them as well. They need to see conflict resolution and grow up with the hope that restoration after conflict brings everyone closer together.

Forgiveness.

Forgiveness is a powerful tool for working through conflict and acknowledges that you are willing to absolve any wrong you or someone else did and move forward. But, like most things, forgiveness can often be misunderstood. Forgiveness doesn't mean the hurt someone causes is okay or that you pretend it never happened. Instead, forgiveness means you acknowledge the wrong and show a willingness to reconcile and create wholeness again. It's not easy because we often remember the hurt, but try your best to not build walls. It's imperative to say the words, "I forgive you," and, "You are forgiven." They bring closure and healing.

As a parent, remember to give yourself grace. You are going to make mistakes. Our spouses, friends, and family will make mistakes. Your kid will make mistakes. But over time, and with care and attention, you can lead your family in healthy ways to interact and work together positively through conflict.

"Babies learn from the verbal and non-verbal cues, postures, and tones used to work through conflict."

Have grace with yourself.

Chapter 76

PARENTING ROLES.

Defining "normal" for your family.

Rebecca Gitlitz-Rapoport (she/her) and **Sam Rapoport** (any pronouns) are a two-mom family living in New Jersey with a three-year-old son and a brand-new baby. Becca is a two-time, Emmy-award-winning documentary filmmaker, and Sam oversees gender diversity efforts in professional football.

2 Kids	Both Gay	Married	White

TL;DR: Parenting looks different for everyone, but families with nontraditional roles—like a home with two moms or two dads—can get bombarded with invasive questions and unwanted input. To navigate any version of nontraditional parenting, be prepared with answers that protect your family's right to thrive.

We are a two-mom household. Our roles in raising our son are not defined by gender norms, societal pressure, or parenting books. We had to choose our own parenting path, and that turned out to be a privilege.

You see, part of the beauty of being gay is that we don't operate in the predetermined roles the world set out for us. We get to work within our individual strengths to choose our own adventure. We have different parenting styles that are complementary. We constantly remind ourselves: "He needs both!"

But when you make your own way, it also draws attention. People asked a lot of inappropriate questions in our first year of parenting, so we've put together a quick cheat sheet for navigating conversations with people who feel the need to indulge in their curiosities.

Our examples apply to a two-mom cisgender* family that did not go the beautiful route of adoption.

*Cisgender means you are a person whose gender identity corresponds with the sex you were identified as having at birth.

To LGBTQIA+ parents: we hope the following guide helps you prepare for what might (but hopefully doesn't) come your way.

To straight cisgender parents:

Take a moment to consider how these categories may line up with your own circumstances which might not be considered "traditional." See these notes as steps toward being a stronger ally of classically "nontraditional" parents.

1. How did it happen?

Example questions:

"Who's the mom? No, the real mom."

"Did you do IVF?"

"How did you pick the sperm donor? Do you know him?"

Why this is problematic:

These are private questions that generally center straightness as "normal." Nontraditional parenting takes a lot of conscious effort and being asked to educate others about your experience can be exhausting, even under the best circumstances.

2. Who does what in your family?

Example questions:

"Does he have male figures in his life? Is his grandfather like a father?"

"But who's going to teach him how to shave and tie a tie?"

"Do you need my husband to teach him about his penis?"

Why this is problematic:
These are not really questions—they're judgments based on the idea that children need a specific parenting scenario to truly thrive.

3. How will baby turn out?

Example questions:

"Does your son have a higher chance of being gay?"

"Will your son ever meet his father?"

Why this is problematic:
These questions are full of harmful and erroneous presumptions—being gay is a choice, a donor is a "father," or a surrogate is a "mother." They also suggest the parents' choices are a problem their child will have to overcome.

How should I answer?

Here are some suggested answers based on how we've handled questions that make us uncomfortable:

"I'm not comfortable answering that question."

"It sounds like you're curious about my experience. Here's what I'm comfortable sharing."

"I'm happy to discuss this with you because we are close, but let's find a time to discuss when I'm not put on the spot."

"I'm not sure what you mean. Could you better explain what you want to know?"

Talking and thinking about how we'll respond to potentially upsetting questions has helped us protect our family's peace and hold our community accountable.

Choosing our roles based on our strengths and weaknesses rather than norms has optimized our marriage and made it stronger. Happy parents raise thriving children. And our kid is thriving!

Remember, no one person's normal is the right normal. Make your own.

"Talking and thinking about how we'll respond to potentially upsetting questions has helped us protect our family's peace and hold our community accountable."

Chapter 77

POSTPARTUM DEPRESSION.

Put your oxygen mask on first.

Patricia A. White is a millennial mama, wife, and influencer who helps moms create a holistic postpartum plan so they can learn to advocate for themselves. Her work helps new mothers make educated decisions postpartum and feel confident within the ambiguities of motherhood.

2 Kids	Married	Haitian American

TL;DR Sometimes after a baby comes depression. Creating a postpartum plan and asking for support allows you to get back to baby, and, most importantly, get back to yourself.

Important note: If you are experiencing symptoms of depression or anxiety, please consult your doctor.

It was 2017 when my husband and I decided to start our family. We had just gotten married, moved away from everything familiar, and each started new jobs in our dream careers. Shortly after we moved, we got pregnant and couldn't be happier. But, a couple months into my pregnancy, things got difficult and I almost lost my baby because of pregnancy complications.

After Carter was born, everything I experienced came crashing down on me. To make matters worse, I felt like I couldn't address my trauma. I thought, How *dare* I complain when I have this perfectly blessed baby boy in my arms!

Postpartum Depression.

But no matter how much I tried to ignore my moods, they expressed themselves in other ways. I didn't feel comfortable leaving the house unless my husband came with me. I had panic attacks, sleep paralysis, and I barely showered because I was afraid to leave my baby alone.

One day, thoughts of unworthiness and hopelessness set me off on a search to find a therapist. During our sessions together, I learned I had postpartum depression and anxiety and struggled with setting boundaries. Since then, I've tried every tool and resource I could find, and I've overcome many of my fears. Through therapy, I learned how to have a smoother and more emotionally balanced postpartum journey.

If you ignore your trauma, avoid therapy, and hold your baby registry in higher regard than your health, this is for you. I encourage you to practice prioritizing your mind, body, and spirit. Start by creating a postpartum care plan.

Here's what your postpartum care plan should include:

- Consult your doctor or midwife to talk about how you're feeling.
- Find a therapist who specializes in perinatal mood disorders.
- Seek out an in-person or virtual mom tribe, so you don't feel alone.
- Consider a meal plan subscription to make your life a little easier.
- Secure a postpartum doula.
- Keep friends and family close by and ready to help.

"If you ignore your trauma, avoid therapy, and hold your baby registry in higher regard than your health, this is for you."

Chapter 78

POSTPARTUM DEPRESSION FOR DADS.

It happens to dads too and it's important to talk about it.

Joel Leon (he/him) was born and raised in the Bronx, New York. He is a proud Black father and girl dad, storyteller, and a creative director at The New York Times. Joel lives to color outside the margins and dismantle systems that oppress our spirits and creativity, by any means necessary.

Heterosexual	Black, African American, West Indian

TL;DR: Fathers experience postpartum depression as well as the shame that comes with it. Understanding and accepting new parenthood as a huge adjustment that impacts everyone differently can open you to healing and unimagined growth.

It was 3:35 a.m. The house was relatively quiet except for the last remnants of a stirring winter clicking its heels against our window—the chill of the night breaking up the oncoming dawn. While my partner tried to rest in our bedroom, a beautiful deep-sleeping baby lay on my chest as I searched endlessly on my phone for an article, a website, a forum, or a chat room that could explain why I didn't want to be around her.

A month and a half after my daughter, West, was born, New York City went under official lockdown to curb a pandemic that most presumed would pass quickly. Two months before that, my eldest daughter, Lilah, moved to Houston with her mother.

In hindsight, the early months of 2021 were some of the roughest I ever had. What exacerbated those months' events was the extreme disconnect and anger I felt toward our newborn baby. This child communicated nothing like Lilah and didn't seem to love or want me the way she did either. What was I doing wrong?

To make things worse, I felt like there was no one to talk to about it. How do you express frustration about a baby you didn't birth or carry in your body for nine months? So much of the shame and guilt behind a father's depression comes from the idea that we should only feel joy and elation. After all, this child shares your eyes, ears, nose, that dimple, or the gap in your teeth.

If someone would have told me I could feel depressed, even angry, about the monumental shift that occurs when bringing a child into this world—regardless of whether it's your first, second, or fifth—maybe I would have been less ashamed to share what I'm sharing now. But I'm hopeful that telling this story will allow other fathers to do the same.

If you are a father or non-birthing parent experiencing postpartum depression or anxiety, here are a few steps to take toward feeling better:

- Talk to a therapist.
- Talk to your partner or co-parent.
- Talk to other dads you know and share your experience. You'll be surprised who can relate.
- In the moments you feel less-than-connected to your child, let your partner know and get some space.
- Ask for help—there is no guilt, shame, or embarrassment in what you're going through.
- Own and admit to your feelings so you can start to heal.

"How do you express frustration about a baby you didn't birth or carry in your bod for nine months?"

Chapter 79

PREPAREDNESS.

Always be prepared to pivot.

Jendayi Keen is a Broadway musical-loving world traveler, designer, and design enthusiast. When she's not working, you'll find her reading a book, frolicking in nature, or planning her next big adventure. She resides in Los Angeles, California, with her husband, son, dog, cat, and new baby on the way.

She/Her	2 Kids	Married	Black

TL;DR: Even the most prepared parent will be met with unforeseen surprises once their baby arrives, and planning to avoid every possible hiccup may prove fruitless in the end. Ultimately, the best thing to prepare for is accepting that we will always be unprepared.

It was six weeks before my due date, and in preparation for bringing my baby home, I focused on checking tasks off my list.

Breastfeeding class: Check.
Assemble crib and changing table: Check.
Interview pediatricians: Check.
Read recommended parenting books: Check.

I live my life as an avid planner, a perpetual list-maker, and a person who loves when things are timely and organized.

Then, at thirty-four weeks and five days, I learned there are just some things we can't plan.

Preparedness.

I woke up to find my water had broken. My husband rushed me to the hospital, where the doctors put me on bed rest. My son was born two days later, healthy, but because of his preterm birth, he was only three pounds, fifteen ounces, and still needed to learn to latch on. The hospital staff immediately took him to the Neonatal Intensive Care Unit (or NICU), our home for the next nine days.

Throughout our stay in the NICU, I told myself, "This is not in the plan, but it's all working out."

I was right.

For example, I realized that being so close to the NICU staff was a blessing in disguise. Before giving birth, I had no experience with babies, but I learned from the experts how to breastfeed properly, pump, swaddle, and bathe my newborn, and other essentials of caring for me and my little one.

The plan going awry taught me my first big parenting lesson that I now pass on to new parents: as much as we prepare, we must also accept the pivot.

"I kept telling myself, 'This is not in the plan, but it's all working out.'"

Chapter 80

STAY-AT-HOME PARENT.

Staying at home is your choice to make.

Wynn Rankin (he/him) is a stay-at-home dad for his two sons. As gay men, he and his husband initially didn't think they could have a family, then they were overwhelmed with the various options and compromises. They stumbled upon the path of using a gestational carrier via some friends pursuing that option, and it's been one of the best, most unique experiences of their lives.

He/Him	2 Kids	Married	White

TL;DR: People have plenty of opinions on staying at home as parents. Rely on your own voice and the thoughts of your team to make the decision that's right for you.

"What does being a stay-at-home parent mean for your *team*?"

That's the question a friend asked me when I was floating the idea of leaving my job to raise our oldest son. It helped me realize that a lot of my thinking was based on exploring other peoples' experiences and I hadn't actually spent much time turning down the volume and taking stock of my own priorities.

I also did a double take with the idea of "team"—a word I've always associated with work. The question helped me realize that my number-one team had quietly shifted to being the group of people who were helping me raise my family, not the ones that were helping me do my day job.

I went back to work at first because I liked my job and was afraid of putting that part of my life on pause. But that job also asked more of me than I was willing to give at the time. It took months for me to realize that even though I was scared of making such a bold shift, I was more scared of missing time with the child I put so much effort into bringing into the world.

My friend's initial question led to a lot more that aided in my decision to stay at home, all of which I think are helpful to ask yourself if you're in a similar position:

- Do I want to stay at home?
- What excites me about staying at home?
- What scares me about staying at home?
- Can my team (aka child-raising group) support it both financially and emotionally?
- How do I keep space for myself?
- How do I make space for others to share the load?

Those last two have been especially important in my own experience. Some people say you can't spend too much time with your kid—I'm not one of those people. If you do end up being a stay-at-home parent, I can't recommend enough to figure out how to let your team support you.

Staying at home feels like a big commitment, but it was helpful to not let anyone else define what it meant for me and my team. It's all about defining balance for yourself and not giving more than you want—to work or to your family—without being intentional about it.

Oh, and please remember you can always change your mind. Or be okay when your mind gets changed for you. With parenting, having a plan is great, but adapting your plan on the fly based on what's actually happening is the real magic.

"My number-one team had quietly shifted to being the group of people who were helping me raise my family, not the ones that were helping me do my day job."

Chapter 81

DIVORCE.

An opportunity to "fail up."

Simona Folasade Sillah is a Los Angeles native who is blooming in Sacramento, California. She is the life guide to her two children, Josiah (8) and Logan (10). Simona makes a point to expand her children's development through travel, community involvement, and encouraging an attitude of inclusion. As a Black woman and mom, Simona spends her free time inspiring women, communities of color, and underserved populations to heal radically through obedience to their mind, body, and spirit—inseparable allies!

She/Her	Partnered	2 Kids	Black

TL;DR: As tough as it is, divorce can lead to better growth, mental well-being, and peace for the whole family, but it comes with challenges as well. Emphasizing extending kindness to yourself and others and adopting the perspective of "failing up" can help you weather this transition with grace.

I divorced three years into my marriage and felt like a complete failure.

My spouse and I reached a point where we were no longer aligned, and we weren't willing to submit to one another or work together to evolve.

We weren't mentally or emotionally equipped to weather the storm of our marriage and remain intact as people. So for the sake of our children and ourselves, we parted ways. Eventually, I started to look at my failed marriage as an opportunity to "fail up" instead of allowing social expectations around marriage and my own ego to beat me down.

Failing up meant instead of wallowing in what was wrong and lost, I chose an optimistic approach. Although our marriage ended, by choosing to divorce, we gained:

- Peace of mind for our children and ourselves
- The opportunity to find better-suited life partners
- Space to get to know ourselves
- The ability to show our children how to choose love consciously

Even with a positive outlook, divorce comes with some big challenges. Navigating divorce while caring for an infant will be tiresome, frustrating, and even hurtful at times. As you move through this next phase of your life as a family, here are a few things to help you get to the other side.

Consider a mediator to work through child-rearing disagreements.

Having an unbiased voice to assist in settling disputes helps remove emotion so you can focus on important decision- making.

Stay optimistic and be intentional.

Divorce has the ability to bring out the worst in just about anyone. Moving in alignment with yourself during this time will make all the difference. Choose your thoughts, words, and actions carefully. Try to remember your littles are listening and watching everything you say and do.

Treat yourself with exceptional kindness and grace.

I wish I understood this early on in my life and marriage. After signing my settlement papers, my own unkindness toward myself bled into the next five years of my life—such a waste of energy. Being kind to yourself sets the tone for how you allow others to treat you. It also fosters deeper levels of peace and confidence in your world—a necessary act in the art of failing up!

Chapter 82

ANXIETY AFTER BABY.

Information is key to understanding the complexities of postpartum anxiety.

Dr. Cassidy Freitas is a licensed marriage and family therapist, mom to three, and hosts the postpartum parenting podcast *Holding Space*. She and her partner felt completely unprepared for the life-altering changes that came with having their first baby. This experience became her muse for shedding light on the not-so-talked-about parts of postpartum: the relationship challenges, the guilt, the shifts in identity, the unexpected symptoms like scary thoughts and irritability. Based in San Diego, California, she supports individuals and couples navigating fertility, loss, pregnancy, postpartum, and beyond.

She/Her	3 Kids	Married	Biracial

TL;DR: Anxiety is a healthy human response when it's functioning to keep you safe. When it starts to impact your day-to-day life, it's gone beyond its helpful, purposeful limits. If postpartum anxiety is a part of your daily existence, reach out to a professional or a person you trust. Be aware of the symptoms in order to get the help you need.

I still remember the first day I was home alone with our three-week-old daughter. We were struggling with breastfeeding and in my sleep-deprived haze, I packed up the diaper bag to attend a local lactation support group.

At the time, we lived on the second floor of a duplex. I walked out the door, took a few steps down, and froze. Staring down at my newborn baby, a graphic image of tripping and falling on her at the bottom of the staircase popped into my mind. A wave of panic flowed from the pit of my stomach to my hands. I felt dizzy. I was afraid I might actually lose my grip. I turned around and walked back inside. Anxiety had impacted my ability to leave the house, and this was the first sign that I needed help.

Your mind is complex and powerful. It can help you plan for the future, learn from the past, and make sense of your experiences. It's also your mind's job to protect you, and as humans, we are wired with emotions such as fear and anxiety.

Becoming a parent can drastically increase your sense of vulnerability. Toss in some sleep deprivation and the overwhelm of caring for a newborn, and it's quite understandable that many new parents experience an increase in anxiety and intrusive, scary thoughts postpartum.

In fact, research has reported that somewhere between ten and twenty percent of birth parents may experience postpartum anxiety (otherwise known as PPA).[1] Considering the stigma around admitting we are struggling when we are "supposed" to be in baby bliss mode, it's very possible even more parents struggle silently with anxiety after the baby arrives.

So, if you find yourself feeling more anxious during this season of life, you're absolutely not alone. Did you know anxiety symptoms can even pop up during pregnancy and non-birth partners are at risk too? The word *symptom* is critical here. Your reactions to anxiety are not *you*, they are symptoms.

You may be wondering: What are the risk factors? What are the different types of anxiety disorders? What are the symptoms? When is it time to get professional support?
Here are a few risk factors to consider:

- A personal or family history of anxiety disorders
- Thyroid imbalance

- History of infertility, pregnancy loss, or stillbirth
- History of an eating disorder
- History of intense mood shifts with menstrual periods
- Limited quality support or community

Types of anxiety disorders that can show up before or after baby and their symptoms:

Generalized Anxiety Disorder (GAD)
- Symptoms include: constant worry, sense of dread, racing thoughts, changes to sleep and appetite, irritability or rage, feeling like you can't sit still, and/or physical symptoms like headache, nausea, and hot flashes.

Panic Disorder (PD)
- Symptoms include: recurring panic attacks where you may experience shortness of breath, chest pain, claustrophobia, dizziness, heart palpitations, and/or numbness and tingling in your extremities.
- Panic attacks will not hurt you but it may be hard to believe that when experiencing one.

Obsessive Compulsive Disorder (OCD)
- Symptoms include: persistent scary thoughts or images that are very disturbing to the parent. These obsessions may be followed by compulsions such as counting, cleaning, or rituals.
- The parent may also experience hypervigilance or fear of being left alone with their baby.

Post-Traumatic Stress Disorder (PTSD)
- Symptoms include: flashbacks, avoidance, hypervigilance, irritability, sensitive startle response, detachment, and anxiety or panic attacks.
- This may be related to traumatic events that occurred before, during, or after birth.

When is it time to get support?

Bringing your worries out of the shadows of your mind and into the light with someone who can hold space for you can be the most proactive and protective step you can take for yourself and your growing family. If you're struggling with any of the above symptoms and it's impacting your relationships or daily functioning, it's time to get help.

Oof, this is a lot to take in, right? I know, but another one of the biggest protective factors is awareness! The good news? If you find yourself struggling with anxiety before or after your baby is born you now know that you are *not* alone and it is absolutely treatable. The tough news? Anxiety is something we are all wired for and it does, at times, serve a purpose. So, it may not go away completely, but it is possible to develop a new and empowering relationship with the protective part of you. If anxiety is stealing the joy of your experience as a new parent, don't wait to get help. Support is out there, and you deserve to feel better.

"Bringing your worries out of the shadows of your mind and into the light with someone who can hold space for you can be the most proactive and protective step you can take for yourself and your growing family."

---

[1]"Maternal and Child Health," Department of Health | Maternal and Child Health | About Perinatal Mood Disorders, March 29, 2017, https://nj.gov/health/fhs/maternalchild/mentalhealth/about-disorders/.

Chapter 83

CO-PARENTING.

Raising a baby with your ex. Yes, it's possible.

Tranette Martin is a thirty-three-year-old mother of three (two daughters and a son). She was born and raised in Albuquerque, New Mexico, and is currently a substitute teacher at a charter school. When Tranette is not driving her kids crazy, she gives back to her community through the nonprofit organization, Seeds Of Sharon.

She/Her	3 Kids	Hispanic

TL;DR Breakups happen, but a family is still a family, even if they live in different houses. Keep the peace by communicating and focusing on supporting a happy and healthy baby.

I had my first child three weeks before turning twenty years old. I was a single mom, but the joy was overflowing and I loved every minute I spent with my baby. Then came the day her dad asked if he could take our daughter to visit his family.

Right away I thought, Absolutely not, she's too little. There was no way he knew how to care for a newborn. But I eventually agreed that a visit for a couple of hours was okay. When the day arrived, my anxiety came rushing in. Did I pack everything in her bag? What if this, what if that? It was exhausting, and once they left, all I could do was count the minutes until her return.

When he brought her back home in perfect condition I realized I had worried for nothing. Instead, I had lost out on some much-needed me-time. The first year was a rough process of figuring out how to co-parent. We tried to sort out schedules, who should pay for what, childcare—you name it, we fought about it. Co-parenting felt so overwhelming and stressful, but as I reflect on that time, my stubbornness was the cause of most of it.

I wanted to control everything and I only trusted myself to lead in the parenting responsibilities. Eventually, I had to take a step back and ask myself if taking on everything was best for our child.

Here are some things I learned as I redesigned a new approach to co-parenting.

Keep it between the parents.
Co-parenting becomes especially difficult when outside parties chime in. Agree to keep decision-making between the two of you.

Share calendars and schedules.
Schedules are amazing! Planning can hold both parents accountable as well as create consistency for your child.

Communication is key.
Over-communicate, be specific, and check in. This makes things so much easier and helps avoid misunderstandings.

Keep it clean.
Co-parenting tends to bring up conflict from time to time, but remember to fight fair. Don't put one another down, especially when tiny ears are in the room.

Talk about new partners.
Parents should make the decision together whether or when new people should meet the baby. There is no perfect time frame; the golden rule is do whatever makes the most sense for your family.

Co-parenting is an emotional roller coaster and you're not always going to agree with each other—that's okay. The most important part of co-parenting is focusing on your child's overall well-being. If you hold that as the main objective, you are already doing an amazing job.

You are a great parent.

Chapter 84

OVERCOMING FRUSTRATION.

Even in our most worn-down state, we have
a choice to respond with love.

Matthew C. Winner lives with his partner and two kids in
Ellicott City, Maryland. He is an educator, a librarian, and
the head of audio at A Kids Co.

He/They	2 Kids

TL;DR: Just because you become a parent doesn't mean you
stop feeling ugly emotions from time to time. You're human, and
your feelings are natural. Draw on the love you feel for the little
one in your arms and meet them where they're at.

*He will not stop crying and you don't know why. There are days
when it feels like he only wakes to nurse and to cry, his skin a map
of red blotches.*

*You will swaddle him and he will keep freeing an arm. And you
will feel the temper trap deep from within yourself.*

*You will move his tiny arm down to swaddle him again and it will
pop back up. Over and over.*

*You will attempt to feed him the breast milk he so desperately
needs, yet so minimally consumes.*

Overcoming Frustration.

The milk that is gold. The milk that takes such great effort for your partner to produce such a limited amount.

And he will cry and cry and cry.

Sleep-deprived and frustrated, I could feel my anger rising with the strength of my baby's cries. I had thoughts I'm not proud of and might be shamed for sharing. To this day, I still wonder if other parents have experienced the same waves of emotions I did in those moments.

The struggle with my temper is one of my defining qualities in that I can see the times I've gone to that edge, but I can also see that I was able to meet the moment with love, however imperfectly.

So, when the baby refuses to swaddle, you may think to
    a.   give way to the temper trap, pushing his arm back in place repeatedly.

But choose to
    b.   look into his eyes. See his hurt. Gently place his arm by his side as often as is needed, or find another way to help him feel secure.

When the baby refuses breast milk or formula—over and over—you may think to
    a.   rigidly hold the bottle in place, refusing to relent your temper to his tears until the milk is consumed.

But choose to
    b.   syringe-feed a few drops, an ounce at a time, seeing him in his hurt and meeting him in his need with love.

And when the tears just won't stop, you may think to
    a.   leave him on a playmat on the floor and just walk away,

OR
    b.   yell at him to stop crying. Curse him. Scream.

But choose to

    c.   do something completely spontaneous because "When all else fails…" And you will hold him as if he is a football, gently rocking. And you will do deep lunges as you gently rock him alongside you.

Sing the Beach Boys' "Wouldn't It Be Nice" and rock and rock until he is asleep. And then you will continue holding him like this.

And your partner will say, "He looks like a tree frog." And you will feel the warmth of his body swell in your arms.

That warmth will dismantle temper's hold. It may come again. But not soon. And not now.

That warmth will dim the light on anything outside of you and him at this moment. Anger dimmed. Shame dimmed. Desperation dimmed.

You will hold him as long as he needs it.

And you will hold this moment forever.

"The struggle with my temper is one of my defining qualities in that I can see the times I've gone to that edge, but I can also see that I was able to meet the moment with love, however imperfectly."

Chapter 85

INTRODUCING YOURSELF TO BABY.

Expose this new tiny person to your world.

Jess Teutonico is a divorced, single soccer mom to Luca in New York City. She is the executive director of We Are Family Foundation, a youth champion, activist, and community builder. She is fascinated by social constructs and contracts. Jess loves dance parties in the kitchen with her son (even his eye rolls), and playlists are her love language.

She/Her	1 Kid	Divorced

TL;DR: You don't lose yourself just because you have kids. It's more important to let your child see just how cool you are. Include your baby in as much of your reality as you can so they learn how to stay passionate about life.

"He's too young. He's just a baby. It will be easier to leave him at home. You should go by yourself." I was constantly met with these words from opinionated loved ones when Luca was born.

Going to an equal rights march. Leave him home. Flying out of the country. Leave him home. Hosting a summit for work. Leave. Him. Home.

But I didn't leave him home. Luca came everywhere with me.

Babies see, hear, and feel everything deeply. So exposure, especially as a new human, is critical. It forms their first opinions of the world, and most importantly, of you.

Somewhere along the way, society whispered in our ears that we need to give up our lives to take on parenthood—or at least keep it separate. To me, this was the most damaging paradigm of all, and I was determined as a new mom not to fall for that trap.

The best thing we can do as parents is to live our fullest lives in front of our children and model what it means to live in joy. Invite them into who we are as people, not just who we are as parents.

If we want to raise children who are secure enough to explore and share their most authentic identity, we need to model our own authentic identity from the start.

Here are some fun activities to help introduce your baby to who you are and to help you stay who you are:

Follow your beat.
Make playlists of your music for your child. Those songs are a story of who you are and are a way of sharing and connecting.

More than baby books.
Don't just make baby books to document your child's life. Make a book about *you* for your child—who you were before you had them and who you are now that they are here.

Pen pals.
When you travel without your child, write them a letter about what you're experiencing, seeing, tasting, and learning. Write as if they were experiencing it with you, and after you put those letters in the mail, put them all in a book just for your baby.

Baby rave.
Invite your friends over for a dance party at home. Those endorphins are contagious (and a great natural boost for sleep-deprived parents).

Book Club.
That stack of unread books you haven't had time to read since they were born? Read them out loud to your baby.

Chapter 86

PARENTING GROUPS.

How to find your people by finding yourself.

Sherisa de Groot is a Brooklyn, New York, native, born and raised. She now lives in Amsterdam, the Netherlands, with her husband, two children, and a cat. Sherisa is the founder of Raising Mothers, a digital space created to celebrate and center Black and brown parenting narratives.

She/Her	Married	Black, Caribbean American

TL;DR: When parenting kicks in, sometimes so does isolation. Whether they are down the block, the next state over, or entirely online, building a community with like-minded folks will help you feel a lot less alone.

When I first became a mom, I had to learn to lean into my vulnerability and allow others to show up for me in ways I wasn't used to. I live more than 3,000 miles away from my family and friends, so online spaces were my best resources. They helped me to align more with how I wanted to parent. I eventually founded an inclusive digital community that centers parents of color, based on the idea that it takes a village to raise us too.

Here are a few things to keep in mind as you look for your people.

There's no wrong way to find community.

Focus on what is important to you right now. Maybe you want to find other parents with babies the same age as yours, or maybe you want to meet more parents who live around you. Don't force it and always stay open to growing with people. You could initially bond over your baby and later discover more shared interests. You may create a community where you least expect it. Embrace it all.

Release your expectations.
In my first year of parenthood, I mourned the shift in my relationships, especially those that ended. However, the people I least expected to were the ones who offered support. Releasing my assumptions created space so I could appreciate those who did show up. Prepare for a shift in your existing community; significant events usually reveal who our folks really are.

Communicate openly.
I learned to openly communicate my needs without shame. You can't do everything on your own, so you have to let others step in. I know I deserve to advocate for myself. You deserve it too. Often, people don't know how to help, so don't be afraid to tell them, even if you just want them to be present.

As your needs change, so can your community.
Change can feel scary, but the joy of finding the right support system is worth it. Stay open to the entire wonderfully awkward process. Make a new friend or rekindle old ones by embracing this new phase of life. Parenting should be a community effort.

"Prepare for a shift in your existing community; significant events usually reveal who our folks really are."

Chapter 87

DOCUMENTING FIRSTS.

Parent your kid beyond the lens finder.

Harold Hughes is a first-generation American raised in a Jamaican household. As a startup founder and dad to Carter and Camryn, he preaches work-life prioritization rather than work-life balance. Harold and his wife, Tiffany, are raising their "Little Leos" in Austin, Texas.

He/Him	2 Kids	Married	Black

TL;DR: When it comes to capturing your baby's firsts, there are no rules. You don't need the latest and greatest in technology— just make the most of the resources you have! And most importantly, don't invest so much of your time and energy in capturing the moment that you forget to live in it.

When I first became a parent, I truly felt like I had no idea what I was doing. Does the baby need to eat? Are we due for a diaper change? Is the swaddle tight enough? While those questions rattled around in my head, I found myself documenting literally everything—in part to make sure I captured baby's firsts, but also to live in those moments longer.

As I write this, I have taken 4,604 pictures of our little Leo, who will be turning five this year. When it comes to capturing memories of your little one, there are no rules, but here are a couple of tips to help make the most of each experience.

Documenting Firsts.

Don't bother with a fancy camera. When I was a kid, my dad was the person in our family always behind a chunky camcorder or tripod. That meant many hours of footage, but rarely did we *see* him. Instead of buying a nicer camera, use your cell phone. The camera quality is great, and the front-facing cameras most phones have offer plenty of opportunities for baby's first selfie.

Use the Cloud—trust me. The quality of pictures on most phones is pretty good these days, so the size of each file can be big. Each of my pictures is about five megabytes, which doesn't sound like a lot, but by the time you get to nearly 5,000 pictures, that's more than twenty gigabytes of data. With cloud storage, you're able to protect your memories from being erased (even when the little one tosses your phone in the toilet) while also saving space on your phone for all those baby-tracking apps you downloaded.

Share moments often. When I was growing up, the only time my relatives would see pictures of us was when my family sent a holiday card or flipping through photo albums on a visit. Now, thanks to technology, we can share precious moments instantly!

We opted for creating a shared album that allowed my wife and me to take pictures and videos of our son which would automatically be shared with grandparents, aunts, and uncles. By leveraging technology to help us capture and share memories, we were able to delight our relatives with baby giggles or a bath time photo and build those family bonds, even when far apart.

Lastly, when it comes to making memories, I want to stress the importance of capturing the moment but also living in it. Don't be the parent who has the phone glued to their hand. Once you snap that picture or grab that ten-second video, put the phone away and enjoy the time with your little one because before you know it, they'll be a bit bigger, and I would hate for you to have missed it by staring into a four-inch piece of glass.

Chapter 88

OVERCOMING OVERWHELM.

Cultivating inner confidence when emotions run high.

Tejal V. Patel is a leading trailblazer in the #kidsCANmeditate movement. She's a mindful parenting coach, author of the award-winning book *Meditation for Kids*, and host of *The Time-In Talks Podcast*. She lives in South Jersey with her hubby, Chirag, three young kids, Ayaan, Rihaan, and Sahana, and their chatty bird, Skye.

3 Kids	Married	South Asian

TL;DR: When you're facing uncertainty or anxiety, there are tools that can help you develop strength from within.

When you're not sure what's right for your child, or if you're doing the right thing, it's easy to fall down the rabbit hole of overwhelm. We frantically scour the internet and anxiously search twenty different sources for what we should do. It's somehow easy to believe other parents and professionals are more informed about parenting than you.

On the other hand, some parents assume that because they have multiple children, they're a parenting pro. But that's not true. I experienced a lot of confusing firsts with my third baby. She was my first to have severe baby acne, latching issues, and get sick as a newborn. I had no idea what to do.

What I can tell you from experience is that there is no universal parenting manual. Each child is unique and has specifically picked you to guide them on their journey.

You are the greatest parenting expert on your child.

We can stop incessant over-searching, over-asking, and over-thinking when we allow our parenting instincts to guide us.

Any time parenting feels overwhelming, it's helpful to have a practice that brings you back to a place of acceptance. Mantras and breathwork are great meditation tools. A mantra is any repeated positive affirmation or phrase used to motivate and inspire you to be your best self. Here are a few I have used both as a parent and a mindful parenting coach:

STEP 1: TRUST
First, you must trust yourself and the wisdom inside you.

MANTRA: Place your hand on your heart, take a breath, and say "I trust my parenting instincts."

STEP 2: FAITH
Next, have faith that a greater power will guide you toward the solution for the highest good for both you and your child.

MANTRA: "Everything is working out, best-case scenario."

STEP 3: STILLNESS
Lastly, we need stillness to hear the wisdom.

The best time to cultivate daily stillness is during nursing, bottle-feeding, or pumping. Turn off the TV, put away the phone, and try this breathwork technique to build calmness and clarity.

4-1-1 BREATH: Take four short sniffs of air through your nose. Hold the breath for a moment and then release in one slow, long exhale through the mouth. Repeat ten times.

Now patiently wait. When you least expect it, a thought will arise that will guide you to the right person, podcast, or book that holds the solution to your problem.

Chapter 89

SINGLE PARENTING FROM A DAD'S POV.

Thoughts on stepping into the sole parenting role.

Brett Moore is a full-time single father to a daughter, Emma. He runs a small software development firm in Portland, Oregon. He enjoys fishing, reading fiction, playing golf, and hanging out with Emma and their cat, Yo-Yo.

He/Him	1 Kid	Single

TL;DR: Single fatherhood has its joys and its own specific challenges. Focus on the love you can surround your child with, and remember to take care of yourself in the process.

Building a relationship with your newborn is a lovely but challenging experience, even more so when you're going it alone. However, as a single father, let me tell you firsthand—if I can do it, you can do it too.

Raising a young daughter as a single parent with no family support in the area was one of the most challenging and humbling experiences of my life. It was intimidating to me to raise a baby daughter without a mother in the home or around at regular intervals as a co-parent.

I'm not going to sugarcoat this—being a single dad comes with its share of difficulty. But it's doable when you focus on your child's specific needs. For example, for me, finding a solid cast of supporting female role models for my daughter was crucial, as was showing her an immense amount of love.

Managing time for yourself is equally as important as spending time with your baby. Perhaps find a hobby that helps take your mind off the stresses of daily life. For my family, time outside of childcare hours was short, so I started running during the workday. I manage to squeeze in a thirty- to forty-five-minute run several times a week, and the effects it has on my mind and stress levels are immense. Running also helps with energy levels at home, enabling me to play with my daughter more actively even after a long day at work.

And dads, there's a catch: Being a single father means raising kids in a world that doesn't always consider you to be a parent. I learned that one of the worst places to be a single dad is airport washrooms. Some are getting more accessible and have family areas, but it's tough—especially for a dad with a daughter—if they don't. There you'll be in the men's room with your child, all your luggage, and usually no changing table. In situations like this, and for much of the single dad journey, you'll have to get creative.

Dads, I wish you the best in your parenting journey. If life finds you in a place where your child needs you to step up and take on the main parenting role early on, I can tell you first hand how incredibly rewarding and enriching that journey can be. It will change your life for the better.

"I'm not going to sugarcoat it—being a single dad comes with its share of difficulty."

Chapter 90

PRESERVING YOUR RELATIONSHIP.

Heads up—babies can be tough on a relationship.

Pastor Keyonn Anthony Wright-Sheppard Sr., is a pastor, husband, and father of three in Brooklyn, New York. He works as a mentor and anti-recidivism specialist for youth. His three children, each from different relationships, are twenty-seven, twenty, and nine.

| Married & Divorced | Black African American |

TL;DR: Whether you are married or single and co-parenting, your relationship will greatly impact your family's harmony.

The relationship that produces a child is as important as the life it produces.

I have multiple versions of the co-parenting relationship: I am married with a child, I have a child with my ex-wife, and I was never married to my eldest daughter's mom. So I learned first-hand how challenging the first year of parenthood can be for a relationship.

The relationship you have as a couple will affect the one you have with your baby. The images of family our kids receive are powerful, even from birth. Those images shape how children later view not only their parents but themselves. Therefore, maintaining a stable environment for your baby's growth and development means investing time in strengthening the relationship that conceived them.

The goal of partnered parenthood is to share the experience of creating a new human being who embodies a little bit of each of you. You get to share in the process of pregnancy together and learn to appreciate not just one another but the entire experience. Now that parenthood has begun, it's time to create a loving environment for your baby to grow up in.

I grew up in a single-parent household, so I lacked a frame of reference for fatherhood. It's hard to aspire to what you've never seen. If a healthy, loving couple raised me, I believe I would have had a better understanding of how to reproduce it. But, I learned not to allow past conditions be my current limitations.

Children need a nurturing environment so they can feel the love in their space. One of life's greatest experiences is when two people who love one another create a family. The reflection of my spouse I see in our child increases our love daily.

Now, I don't live in a fantasyland. Every couple who conceives won't live happily ever after together. In that case, it's important to keep the co-parenting relationship strong regardless of where the romantic relationship ends up. Your child will recognize your character and be appreciative. Healthy co-parenting is possible when you focus on the love you both have for your baby instead of the issues between the parents.

When you create something this valuable together, prioritize building, growing, loving, and enjoying it together as partners.

"The relationship you have as a couple will affect the one you have with your baby."

Chapter 91

MINDFULNESS.

Finding mindfulness and purpose in parenting, even when all seems lost.

Michael Booth is a graduate of Portfolio Center in Atlanta, Georgia. He is now a freelance writer and designer and stay-at-home father of three: Oliver (7), Irina (3), and Tommy, who passed shortly after birth and would have been eight this year. Michael and his wife, Khristina, were high school sweethearts and recently celebrated their thirteenth wedding anniversary.

He/Him	3 Kids	Partnered

TL;DR: Parenthood involves facing challenges we weren't prepared for—both day-to-day and unimaginably tragic. However, the practice of mindfulness helps parents find peace in the midst of chaos and helps babies grow into kids who can focus on hope in stressful situations.

Trigger Warning: In this work, the author shares information which may be sensitive to some readers.

Even with the perfect pregnancy, things don't always go perfectly. My wife and I lost our son Tommy in 2013 from septic shock, a very rare sickness that happened seven hours after his birth. My wife and I sat in a small room with our family in tears. In my mind I thought, "Did the doctor really say our newborn son died?"

"Out of sight, out of mind," is a phrase often used to mean if we can't see, hear, or sense something, it won't fully exist in our focused mind. This can become a type of coping mechanism for hiding from our obstacles. But they are still there. Quietly waiting to be overcome.

Heartbroken and depressed, my wife and I went through months of counseling that bandaged our broken hearts and helped us eventually find the right coping tools. One of those tools, mindfulness, allowed us to accept the tragedy and find hope.

Hope, Safety, and Sanctuary.

One night, I stood staring up at the night sky. It was like a weighted blanket. A sanctuary for my wife and me. Song lyrics came through my headphones about a galaxy and someday finding someone lost there. It reminded me I would find Tommy again somehow, but for now, I needed to focus on the present, without judgment or regret. My attention was drawn to the knee-high grass, the warm southern air, the mosquitoes biting at my ankles. This practice of noticing my surroundings helped me focus on the years to come as I faced new challenges and adventures with Tommy's younger siblings, Oliver and Irina.

Responding with Purpose.

Self-reflection can help us understand our triggers and coping mechanisms. Responding with purpose helps parents, as well as our children, prepare for spontaneous obstacles without negative emotions. Being mindful people and leading by example helps parents show their children how to respond in stressful situations. As parents, we can relieve moments of mental drain and chaos with watchfulness, meditation, and taking time for ourselves.

Set aside time to do activities you enjoy. I have been playing the drums since I was a kid, and I continue to play them because it brings me joy. I play music because it is a part of me, and I can focus on it and get lost in it. I play music because it's the essence that defines me. Having access to joy provides relief for the mind and brings us back to ourselves. This could be running, creating music, or even skateboarding.

As parents, we spend so much time with our children that we can feel defined by the role of mom or dad. By focusing on the present moment and calmly acknowledging and accepting your feelings, you will be practicing mindfulness. Just be there for yourself and your children and try your best to be you.

And remember, you don't have to be perfect to be a perfect parent. As parents, we have one role: show up and be present, both physically and mentally.

"Being a mindful parent and leading by example helps parents show their children how to respond in stressful situations."

Chapter 92

POSTPARTUM SUPPORT.

A five-minute crash course for the postpartum parent.

Kayla Cushner is a Certified Nurse-Midwife (CNM) in Santa Cruz, California. She graduated from Yale School of Nursing in 2013 with a masters in midwifery and has practiced as a CNM in various hospitals. She is an East Coaster at heart, but has lived in California for the last five years. Kayla lives with her husband, their two young sons, Arlo and Rivers, and their dog named Moose.

She/Her	2 Kids	Married

TL;DR: Postpartum is much bigger than depression. Knowing what to expect in life after birth can equip you to combat the exhaustion and mixed emotions associated with being a new parent.

My experience with postpartum is both personal and professional. As a midwife, I guide patients through postpartum anxiety and depression. In addition to that, after having my first son, I was on the go immediately, which took a toll on me, my relationships, my body, and, most importantly, my mental health.

After my second son was born, I did things very differently. Taking the time to rest, bond with my baby, and fully recover made a huge difference.

For example, after having my first son, I went shopping two days after giving birth because I didn't trust my husband to get the "right" baggy sweatpants. After I had my second son, I took my own advice about rest and accepting support.

I share the following information with my midwifery patients and friends to help them avoid what I experienced. When we don't talk about postpartum planning and support, it affects birthing people, families, babies, and communities in the long run.

- Postpartum is a season of your life that can last about a year as your body heals, but is also long-term—you will always be a new version of yourself, forever changed by your baby who was inside your body and is now their own person.
- Prepare for postpartum similarly to how you prepare for birth. Postpartum will last a lot longer than birth.
- A rule for rest: two weeks in bed and two weeks on the couch. You grew and birthed a human and are now keeping them alive. You also have a dinner-plate-sized open wound in your uterus. So rest for a few weeks. Your pelvic floor, and your future self, will thank you.
- Along with healing, your role in the world is changing. Feeling like the world is a little different now is normal.
- Babies are cute and tiny, but there's a real human in there. Keep your environment quiet and calm so it's easier to listen and get to know their needs.
- Stock up on warm and easy-to-digest foods.
- Say "yes" to the meal train from friends and family. Leave a cooler on your porch for drop-offs.
- Choose who is in your postpartum bubble. It's sacred, so try not to pop it for as long as you can. It's okay if you don't want someone to come over or hold your baby. They'll get over it.
- A warm bath every day for the first month is healing and a welcome five minutes.
- Postpartum life feels like walking around with a layer of skin peeled off. Normal things are overstimulating. Focus on experiences that are simple and feel good.
- Find someone who has a baby around the same age.

It's less lonely.

- You'll feel like you're constantly feeding, which is accurate. Keep your baby skin-to-skin, and feed them when they seem interested or fussy, even if you just fed them.
- Buy cooling pads for sore nipples.
- It's normal if your baby won't sleep on anything but you. There are safe ways to co-sleep if that is what works for your family. Talk with your doctor or midwife about it.
- Smell your baby's head. Snuggle your tiny newborn. And don't listen to people who say, "It goes by so fast," because it will just make you anxious.

When people hear the word "postpartum" they often think "postpartum depression," when really, I think we all need to be thinking "postpartum support." The rest, care, and support that a postpartum family gets in those early months have ripple effects on their lives, the lives of their babies, and on the community.

Let's bring into light the importance of this time and start educating people about it BEFORE they are in the trenches.

"Prepare for postpartum similar to how you prepare for birth. Postpartum will last a lot longer than birth."

Chapter 93

DIVISION OF LABOR.

A different approach to dividing the tasks of parenthood.

Kirby Winfield is a Seattle native who has spent twenty-five years working in technology startups and venture capital. He's been married to his wife, Alison, for twenty-one awesome, roller-coaster years, raising a fourteen-year-old son and a twelve-year-old daughter with Down syndrome.

He/Him	2 Kids	Married

TL;DR: At the beginning of your parenting journey, it's helpful to make decisions that will guide how you care for your partner and how each of you will care for your child.

In 2006, we brought our newborn son home from the hospital during a winter storm in Seattle. The power was out, the temperature in our house was below freezing, and all we were focused on was keeping him alive.

That's your natural instinct as a parent, to react to their needs and do what it takes to help them thrive. All of your fancy plans will soon be forgotten. But before you let nature take over, it's worth it to make a few conscious decisions about parenting first.

One thing we as a couple leaned into was putting our relationship first, right off the bat. Your feelings for your newborn and your reactions to being a parent are intensely personal. Every parent will experience feelings unique to them. The default position becomes, *I am gonna do whatever it takes to keep this kid safe and help them grow*, rather than, *I am gonna do whatever it takes to support my partner and make sure we're providing a safe, happy, and solid environment for our kid.*

Making space for common ground is key and can yield benefits you may not anticipate. For example, we found a babysitter almost immediately so we could have a weekly date night. This seemed selfish to us at first, because we thought of it as something for us and not for our son's benefit.

But as the months and years went by, we realized we'd helped our son feel comfortable around others at an early age. When he got a bit older, not only could we leave him on weekends for much-needed getaways to reconnect as a couple, but we saw him interact naturally with people in new situations. Who knew the simple decision to stick to a weekly date night would help our son become an independent child?

Now, we had some key misses early on that took a long time to dig ourselves out of. In the beginning, there's a temptation to do it all. I'd work at my startup all day, then come home and take the night shift for feeding and changing our baby boy. It wasn't sustainable, and it wore me down and made me resentful. Keeping track of the tasks I took on was poison that trickled in on day one and lasted for years.

The healthy habit we should have formed was to create a flexible approach to sharing the load. Rather than assigning iron-clad roles, we should have taken turns with overnight and daytime care. It's much easier to avoid contempt and frustration when you and your partner take on the same responsibilities on different days—this creates empathy and limits the scorekeeping.

As new parents, you'll unconsciously set up long-term roles and responsibilities that will define your family's journey. Be mindful of that!

Don't focus so much energy on creating static job functions. It feels tempting, but you may wake up ten years later and realize you're only seen as the disciplinarian or the breadwinner, and your relationship with your kid won't be what you want, and you'll resent your partner for that.

It's much better to spend the first year exploring how it feels to each of you to be in charge of whatever comes up—feeding, diapering, physical care, doctor appointments, finding childcare, buying early development toys, researching daycare, choosing the bedtime music—and adopting jobs collaboratively.

"Making space for common ground is key and can yield benefits you may not anticipate."

Chapter 94

ASKING FOR HELP.
The other "H" word.

Sarah Beck is a divorced, single mother to twins James (11) and Andrew (11), who are both on the autism spectrum. She has a beautiful dog named Iris, and in her free time you can find Sarah painting large canvases in her garage.

She/Her	2 Kids	Single	Divorced

TL;DR: While new parents may be determined to do everything they can to take care of their babies alone, when the situation feels dire and you feel like you can't go on any longer: Ask. For. Help.

Adjusting to newborn twins is an arduous process that is both physically and emotionally draining. However, despite the challenges, having twins is an indescribable experience that makes everything worth it.

By day ten of pumping and feeding newborn twins, I felt like I had been run over by a semi truck.

My husband at the time was a tax auditor. It wasn't busy season, so he could help me with our children late in the evenings. We were also able to hire a nanny for weekday mornings, so I could get some sleep. The rest of the time, my plan was to sleep one hour every two or three hours to get at least a combined eight hours of sleep within a twenty-four-hour period.

It didn't go well.

After a week and a half of poor, inconsistent REM sleep and signs of postpartum depression, I found myself sitting on the floor at 4:00 a.m., pumping and bottle-feeding two screaming babies. My preemies struggled to latch on to my breasts and they were both losing weight quickly. I pumped milk into bottles to track how much they were drinking, never able to produce enough milk to store.

I didn't know what to do. I dialed the on-call advice nurse at my doctor's office and begged her for help. I explained my current state of mind and said, "I am afraid I might hurt myself or the babies." She reassured me I was okay.

She calmly said, "You're not going to hurt your babies. People who are a danger to their children generally do not call for help. They pretend everything is fine and make very poor decisions as a result of their lapse in judgment."

The on-call nurse advised me to get on antidepressants immediately, solicit additional help from friends and family, and switch from pumping breast milk to introducing formula. I took all her advice and after a few weeks, I felt like a new person.

At a doctor's visit with my twins, I sought out that nurse. I wanted her to know I was very grateful for her guidance and over-the-phone support because she truly saved us that night.

Accepting my limitations was a necessary first step in asking for help. It was difficult to let go of control, but once I did, I was a healthier, happier, and more well-adjusted mother to my twins. And I had time and energy to enjoy and nurture my beautiful babies as they grew up.

So, now a question: How are you? If you've told yourself everything is fine when you know it isn't, it's time to ask for help.

"Accepting my limitations was a necessary first step to asking for help."

Chapter 95

RETURN TO WORK.

Going back to work does not make you a bad parent.

Sara Scott-Curran is a global citizen living near Portland, Oregon. She is the proud mama to Skyler Everly (12) and wife to Stewart. Her family is her joy, but her career is her calling. Sara spends her free time running half-marathons and (countless) errands.

She/Her	1 Kid	Married

TL;DR: Sometimes the very thing that brings you closer to your growing baby is a little space to shine on your own. If you choose to go to work, it's okay to stick by your choice, but prepare for the big feelings.

When I had my daughter, the plan was always to return to work. And yet, as the time grew closer, the feelings I had about it became unexpectedly messy and complicated.

I was sad, and it was hard, but I knew that going back to work was right for me. To be the best parent I could be, I had to honor my own needs, which meant returning to work and pursuing my career goals. I wanted to lead by example and make Skyler proud.

When the day came to return to work, I handed her off at the daycare, then I cried, and she cried. And then she stopped crying, but I didn't. I cried in the car, in the parking lot, in the elevator. And then something shifted.

For the first time in six months, it was just me. Of course I missed my daughter, but it was liberating to eat lunch with both hands and talk about something other than diapers.

When I picked Skyler up from daycare, she was happy and smiling. All of my worries and fears were totally unfounded. My baby was adaptable and at ease. Even though we had an emotional start to our first day, it ended up being a great day for both of us.

As you embark on your journey as a working parent, you are going to feel a lot of feelings. Excitement, sadness, fear, guilt, and happiness. Not just when you return to work, but as you try to balance all your ever-changing responsibilities.

There will be days where you are crushing it, and there will be days where "it" is crushing you. Much like being a parent, going back to work is a shape-shifting adventure.

Feel it all and keep going. Trust yourself and remember why you're doing it. Every day you do your best is a success, even if your best looks different every day.

When your kiddo gets older and starts to show a deeper interest in what you do or talk about their own career ambitions, you'll be proud. You showed them how to dream big because you did.

You did that. You did it all.

"There will be days where you are crushing it, and there will be days where "it" is crushing you."

Chapter 96

TRAVELING WITH BABY.

How to shed your first-time flight fears.

Tanya Hayles is an award-winning creative storyteller who uses various mediums to evoke emotions, create change, build movements, and bring color to white spaces. In 2015, she started Black Moms Connection to create a safe space for Black mothers to share and connect. It has since grown to an online global village of over 20,000, from Asia to Atlanta.

She/her	1 Kid	Single	Black

TL;DR: Flying with a baby may seem like mission impossible, but this mom shares six helpful tips loaded with encouragement for the most efficient and stress-free traveling experience with baby.

I know. The idea of getting on a plane with a baby either has you wanting to roll your eyes or freeze in fear. You worry about how much stuff is "too much stuff" to bring and what happens when baby cries and "disturbs" the other passengers.

I get it. These hesitations and questions are real and valid. Oftentimes, we, as parents of newborns, feel judged from the moment we step out of our homes. But if you're going to be judged and have folks wishing for an adult-only airline, wouldn't you rather be on your way somewhere sunny?

My son's passport picture was taken when he was a chubby eight-month-old. Once I realized the clock was ticking on free flights for lap-sized infants, I decided to take advantage while I could. My family lives in Canada, but my son's godmother and pseudo-aunties are across the border in the US and were all excited to meet him.

Surprisingly, traveling with my infant son was easier than I thought. He was in a front-facing carrier where he fed and slept for most of the trip. Even though he was expected to stay on my lap, the flight attendants moved me to a seat with an empty one beside it, which lowered my fears by about ten notches. I pack pretty efficiently, so big things like pack-and-plays were borrowed once we arrived at our destination—one less thing to carry and risk breaking.

So, here are my top six tips for traveling with a baby:

Ask for help.
As a single mom, that's something I seem to only do under extreme duress. But from the driver to airport valets to both gate and flight attendants—folks will want to help you because the cargo you are carrying is irreplaceable and way more valuable than anything that's been checked in.

B or B: Breast or bottle.
Have both at the ready from takeoff to descent. While breastfeeding took the pressure off needing to prepare bottles, bottle-feeding parents should not hesitate to ask flight attendants for assistance (hot water) as needed.

Take less, rent more.
The idea of underpacking while traveling with a baby? Seems like mission impossible. But before you go, ask your travel carrier, rental car company, and hotel what they have that you don't need to travel with. This could range from pack-and-plays or playpens at the hotels, to car seats at the car rental company.

Planning makes perfect.
If you truly can't part with the comforts of home, ship baby gear

to your final destination prior to your departure. Or order online and have it delivered.

Choose time over money (if your budget allows).

It's tempting to choose your travel budget over booking a non-stop flight, but dealing with two takeoffs and two landings is twice the amount of work. This, of course, depends on your destination and other financial factors, but it's something I'd seriously suggest considering if you are able.

Be unapologetic.

An airplane is a public mode of transportation. From mouthy teens to obnoxious drinkers and loud talkers, a flight can have all types of characters. Don't be sorry for having a brand-new human being who only knows one way to communicate.

Travel could and should be fun. Traveling is about creating memories that last a lifetime. Whether the purpose is for fun or obligation, try to enjoy it.

"Oftentimes, we, as parents of newborns, feel judged from the moment we step out of our homes."

Chapter 97

THE JOURNEY OF SINGLE PARENTHOOD.

Everything is going to be okay.

Hilary Powers is a white mother to a biracial boy. She was a Peace Corps volunteer in Nicaragua from 2014 to 2016 where she taught entrepreneurship and met her son's father. She currently lives in Atlanta with a wonderful friend network while her son's father remains in Nicaragua. Hilary chose to be a single mom despite the known struggles because she knew this little boy was something she couldn't live without.

She/Her	1 Kid	Single	Heterosexual

TL;DR: Yes, it is just you and your kid in this world. You are the boss of both of you for now, and that is a big job. Find time for each of you and trust in yourself.

Being a single mom sometimes comes with a negative stigma that's tough to overcome. Not only are you navigating this new life and identity, but you are solely responsible for another human being. All the decisions you make from this point forward will feel heavier.

But I'd like to tell you something I wish someone told me—own the decisions you make as a parent and don't let anyone question them, including yourself. Owning your decisions means doing the work and then standing by it and also trusting yourself to know when you need a second opinion. Negativity and judgment from other people can muddle your parenthood experience, which is entirely your own.

No one has been exactly where you are, so their opinions are not your business. I remember feeling frustrated when partnered parents would tell me how much they could relate to my experience, when I knew that wasn't exactly true. And I learned it's okay to feel frustrated by that. Your experience might be really challenging, but remember it's not a competition. Parenthood is hard for everyone.

Regarding parenting partners, it's okay to miss a partner you once had or wish you had one to begin with. Wanting a parenting partner doesn't make you weak or less capable as a single parent—it makes you human, with human feelings.

One positive thing I've found to be helpful as a single mom is to protect my family time. I split our time into three parts: yours, mine, and ours. Time that's focused on my son having fun, like the zoo or the park, is the "yours" time. Time that's focused on bringing me joy or energy, like grabbing margaritas with friends, is "mine". And time that's focused on bringing my son and me together over shared experiences, such as mealtimes and bedtime stories, is "ours". I found this mindset keeps away the mom guilt and the burnout and gives us both a little bit of everything we need in this life.

"I find it really healthy to split our time into three parts: yours, mine, and ours."

Chapter 98

NEW FAMILY DYNAMICS.

Make space to enjoy each other.

Maurice Cowley is a husband, father, and poet who also has a full-time job. He lives in Portland, Oregon, with his wife, Leslie, five children, and one granddaughter. When he finds the time, he loves writing poetry, roasting coffee, and working out.

He/Him	5 Kids	Married	Black

TL;DR: Never stop communicating with your partner and make space to enjoy each other as people. Growing your family is never easy—but it's always worth it.

"I just don't understand how y'all do it."

This sentence has been uttered by just about every one of our friends as we welcomed more children into our family.

Our response? It's always the same: "We make space to enjoy each other."

My wife and I started as two bright-eyed young people in a five-hundred-square-foot apartment. Within a year, we began our parenting journey, which now includes:

- Welcoming a teen who needed to escape an unhealthy home situation.
- Taking in one of our former students while she established herself at a local university.

- Giving birth to twin boys.
- Fostering a teen boy through the Department of Human Services (or DHS).
- Giving birth to our youngest son.
- Fostering and then adopting our daughter, who is six months older than our youngest son.
- Welcoming a student who came to the United States as an unaccompanied minor. She still lives with us and now has a daughter of her own.

This list doesn't include the numerous times people have moved into our home and participated in our family life. It's been a proverbial revolving door of occupancy.

So, how have we done it? It's not that we're more amazing than other couples, because we aren't. Allow me to share our not-so-secret secrets for navigating an expanding family.

From the very beginning, my wife and I made space to enjoy each other. We laugh together a lot. We make time to talk every day: small talk, deep talk, details of life talk. We go on dates, even if the only date we can find time for is a home-cooked meal after all the kids have gone to sleep, or drinks in the backyard, or a quick board game before bed. We cuddle a lot.

Our family started with just us: best friends who fell in love— that part was easy. Making it through what came next required maintaining our friendship and choosing to love each other even when it's hard to. Finally, it required us to forgive each other when we messed up.

Every expansion of our family has motivated us to tend to our love and friendship while sharing it with each new family member we welcome. It has never been easy. But it has always been worth it.

"From the very beginning, we have made space to enjoy each other."

Chapter 99

BODY EMPOWERMENT.

Meet your beautiful new body.

Elle Pierre is a California-bred vocalist, songwriter, make-up artist, and model. She is the mother of a bright boy whom she lovingly refers to as "PB" (short for "poo booty"). Elle lives in Brooklyn, New York, where you may find her frolicking barefoot in the park, practicing yoga, dancing, or enjoying local cuisine.

She/Her	1 Kid

TL;DR: If you are a birthing parent, your body has endured a lot of changes over the last year. Now it's time to get reacquainted and free yourself of the pressure to look exactly the way you did before pregnancy. After all, appreciating your new, beautiful body is the most crucial "snap back."

The conversation around women's bodies seems to be one that people love to engage in. From adolescence, there's a lot of focus on our shape, attire, weight, body hair, sexuality—you name it. Unfortunately, early body-shaming causes some of us to subscribe to impossible beauty standards throughout the rest of our lives. After carrying a human in your womb and experiencing labor, your body is somehow expected to snap back.

In 2016, I gave birth to my son and afterward, adjusting to my new body proved to be quite the feat. My belly stretched during pregnancy, and I had the marks and loose skin to prove it. My belly button was destroyed. I hardly recognized the body that looked back at me in the mirror.

It took time, but I learned to appreciate my mom-bod. Here are some tips to help you do the same.

Rest is more than just an energy refuel.
Motherhood asks a lot of you, so you will need all the emotional and mental support that sleep has to offer.

Choose your look intentionally.
Embrace whatever curves pregnancy supplied by shopping for clothing that compliments your new figure.

Strip down and walk around naked.
Go ahead and take nudes just for you and find beauty in the areas you may be tempted to label unattractive.

Return home to yourself.
An identity crisis is a common postpartum experience. Engage in activities that remind you who you are.

Move your new body.
Try yoga, take an aerial silks class, go rollerskating, have sex. Do whatever it takes to get those endorphins flowing and boost your mood and energy levels.

Remember that your body kept you and your baby safe while you performed the miraculous act of gestation and birth. So be kind, give thanks, and know that you're beautiful, new curves and all.

"After carrying a human in your womb and experiencing labor, your body is somehow expected to snap back."

Chapter 100

MENTAL HEALTH.

Dads feel the pressure to be perfect too.

Homero Radway is the father of three amazing artists: Blu, Moxie, and Glory. He founded Quarks, a family production company specializing in audio and visual art through a Black Queer lens, with his partner, Noleca. Homero is a financier, producer, writer, podcaster, and actor. His family can be heard on the podcast *Raising Rebels*.

He/Him	3 Kids	Married	Black

TL;DR: Nothing challenges your mental health quite like new parenthood. Sifting through the myriad of emotional ups and downs can distract you from the main event—watching your baby grow and learn. Remember your own mental health has a huge impact on how you can show up for your family.

Eleven months into being a first-time dad, I was home alone with my beautiful baby, Blu. As I watched the end of a football game, Blu stumbled around, newly walking, sucking on the bottle I gave her so I could focus on the game. She walked in front of the television and began to fall, and I couldn't reach her in time. My brain signaled me to save her by catching her with my foot. It was like something out of a Kung Fu movie. She ended up tripping over my leg and falling face-first on the floor, screaming. I picked her up and realized her tooth was chipped by the fall.

I cried and hugged Blu while my mind turned to all the ways I was a bad dad. As the sadness and guilt and shame bubbled up, my ego took over, dissociating and numbing me from all of my feelings by the time my partner arrived home.

At the time, I was overworked, stressed, feeling inadequate, and depressed. On top of that, I was mourning my mother's death. As a new father, I felt a lot of pressure to be a better dad than the one I had.

Over time, however, I learned to prioritize my mental health so I could show up for myself more, which allowed me to show up better for my family. Here's what I've learned:

Trust that your children will fall.
I was not going to save Blu with my foot. She just needed me to be there to pick her up, hold her as she cried, and remind her that everything was going to be okay.

Be present.
I was not in the room with Blu. I was miles away at a football game. Being present allows me to be in tune with my children's needs and their movements.

Be compassionate with yourself.
With compassion, I would have processed my shame and guilt and gotten the support and love I needed in order to move past it.

Process your emotions.
I process shame, guilt, and sadness in therapy, which helps me understand how my triggers rub up against being a father.

Share your story.
I share my stories and all of who I am with Blu, Moxie, and Glory, so they can know a part of me that is intimate and vulnerable.

Be vulnerable.
Be open and vulnerable and tell your baby your story. You are worthy of all the love bestowed upon you by your children, partner, family, and friends.

ABOUT THE COMPANY.

A Kids Co. is a new kind of media and commerce company, empowering a generation of kids through diverse storytelling. Launched in 2019, we create kids media and original IP across verticals, including publishing, podcasting, TV/Film, and video, focusing on telling the most important stories kids ever encounter.

ACKNOWLEDGEMENTS

This book exists because of the incredible work of the A Kids Co. team. Each and every member, from our editors to executives, had a hand in making this book happen. This team shows up every day to empower the next generation through diverse storytelling, and this book represents the fullest vision of that mission.

I'd like to give special acknowledgement to this book's designer, Rick DeLucco. His sense of pacing, layout, and style turned this into something truly special. She is noted elsewhere, but the driving force behind this book's completion was Jennifer Goldstein. She worked tirelessly to improve it on every level. Ashley Simpo, Emma Wolf, and Wynn Rankin worked with each contributor as editors to craft honest and authentic wisdom and advice, which you can find on every page.

Lastly, I'd like to thank every single one of our 100 contributors. These are your stories, and we are grateful to get to share them with the next generation of parents.

Jelani Memory
Founder & CEO
A Kids Co.

SPECIAL THANKS.

A very special thanks to D'Rita and Robbie Robinson for their tremendous support, investment, and many introductions.

Thanks to Dr. Becky Kennedy, who introduced us to many of our contributors.

And deep thanks and gratitude to those who are and have been on our team who helped make this project what it is along the way: Megan Laney, Denise Morales-Soto, Alexina Shaber, Savannah Kan, Kenya Feldes, Yazmin Macias, Melanie Wilkins, Amber Weyers, Nakita Simpson, Matthew C. Winner, Jennifer Goldstein, Kennedy Gregory, Kelby Johnson, Louis Halley II, Gabby Nguyen, Catherine Petru, Emma Wolf, Duke Stebbins, Rick DeLucco, Kehlay Luchaco, Chris Arth, Ari Mathae, Stephen Green, Erin Jeffries, Micah Mew, Nygel Jones, and Laki Karavias.

100 Diverse Voices on Parenthood

Designed and typeset by Rick DeLucco
Book printed and bound by Ingram Spark

Composed in Galano Grotesque designed by René Bieder
and Utopia Std designed by Robert Slimbach

Printed on 50#

Distributed by A Kids Co.

THEME KEY.

 Building community & involving other people.

 Single parenting & feeling less alone on this new journey.

 Big topics & speaking up.

 Breast milk & formula.

 The power of love, presence, & nurturing.

 Self-care.

 Development for you & baby.

 Taking a closer look & asking questions.

 Parenting philosophy & gaining a bigger perspective.

 Finding your way & trusting your instincts.

 Diapers, diaper bags, & poop.

 Exploring the world around you for you & your baby.

 Sleep time & nighttime patterns.

 Back to work & staying at home.

 Capturing moments & celebrating milestones.

 Growing in flexibility & getting creative.

 Being outside & connecting with nature.

 Technology & gadgets.

Money & budgeting.

Preparedness & health.

 Growing, changing, & shifting family dynamics.

 Anger & arguments.

 Power Piece.

 Baby.

Notes

Notes

Notes

CPSIA information can be obtained
at www.ICGtesting.com
Printed in the USA
BVHW061605281022
650511BV00006B/22